Elsie,

Dance like
no one is on you
watching or you
become the
beautiful
being "you"

DANCING

With Your Story

From The Inside Out

Published by Richter Publishing LLC www.richterpublishing.com

ISBN: 1945812060

ISBN-13: 9781945812064

Everyone has a story. This book belongs to those who have an open heart and are eager to learn and grow from their stories by being aware, honest, and willing to see the truth. This book is not about the *story*, it is about being courageous enough to move past the story and being you.

DISCLAIMER

Contents

Foreword

Within every person lies their own life story, with their own unique interpretation of past and present events. Over time, we add meaning to these events and create our own stories. Eventually, our interpretations become perceptions that prescribe our outlook on life. But sometimes, as humans, we can make up or misinterpret certain events or situations and become the captive of our own misguided perceptions, while our *real* identities remain trapped inside us.

Arielle Giordano empowers you to "dance your story from the inside out" by freeing yourself through dancing, so that you may finally release your authentic truth and break the shackles of silence with your body's natural rhythms. At the end of each chapter, Giordano offers personal journaling and conscious reflection in conjunction with free-spirited dance. Giordano prescribes a practical means to self-discovery through fun and creative expressions.

Together, the journaling, reflection, and dance assignments help unlock our stories and set our true selves *free*.

—Tara Richter
President of Richter Publishing LLC

Introduction

Hide and Seek

As children, we played the game of hide-and-seek. Players conceal themselves in a place to be found by the seekers. The one player tagged as "it" closes their eyes and counts to a predetermined number while the other players hide. The designated "it" runs and looks everywhere, seeking the other players. In the hide-and-seek game in life, you are "it." You are the one you have been hiding from and seeking your whole life.

My story of being "it" began with the realization that what we see outside ourselves can be a mirror reflection of what is inside. I knew I was "it" after more than ten years of being with the "teacher of truth." I gave up my life as I knew it. I painfully let go of my husband, my dog, my favorite car, my guidance counselor position, and my house. Everything changed, and I did not know or understand why. My old life, as I knew it, changed to a new one. Every cell in my body lit up, sparkled, and danced with the knowledge and realization to move forward. I love to evolve, grow, and learn.

One of my greatest aha moments was the realization that all of my evolution and growth was not only a result of being with my teacher. I, too, was responsible for my growth, evolution, integration of knowledge, and healing. I became deeply aware of aspects hidden deep within me. Patterns and experiences, thoughts and feelings would surface from the subconscious floor and unconscious mind. I learned that when difficulties arise and I feel uncomfortable, a new level within me is surfacing. Each new level triggered new "stuff" within to be looked at, integrated, and healed. My being was resonating in the awareness of who I am as expanded conscious awareness. I experienced a subtle shift in knowing who I am as a being. I learned that everything in life is an opportunity to heal and grow, whether it feels good or not. If a person is nice or not so nice to us, we can grow. If a relationship works or does not work, empowers or enslaves us, we can grow. Every experience in our life is an opportunity to shift awareness and consciousness. We get to choose.

By being truthful about our life stories, we shift. When the beliefs that shape who we are to what we are change, we transform. My life story has changed with the realization that I made up the story. When I consciously made a choice to look at my story differently, I changed and so did my way of being. I realized I created stories about my dad living to see me grow up, and I imagined how different life would have been. But guess what, that did not happen, and he did not live to see my fourteenth birthday. I know now that the deep pain propelled me forward to learn how to enjoy my life without a story and without him. The willingness to accept the truth began my journey of healing.

Dance

Dancing is in your body, stories are in your mind! Stories such as our life experiences are also in every body cell. Dance provides an opportunity to communicate each chapter with our bodies. Let your body move and flow freely as you listen to the music and think and the chapter topic. Dance takes you out of your mind and into your body! Babies dance when they hear music. Be childlike, listen to the music and dance with abandon. You may feel embarrassed, but let yourself move through your resistance or hesitation. Put on your favorite music and dance like nobody is watching. Dance your story from the inside out with movement, creativity, and fun. Let go and set yourself free! Remember, there are no rules. It is not about the way you look right now. You are dancing from the inside out and giving it form. What are you experiencing in your body, what are your feelings and thoughts? Let your body help you to find and release your story!

Writing and Dance Reflection

Each chapter has a section to express and communicate your sensory experiences, thoughts and feelings, and reflect through dance and writing. I recommend that you participate in the suggested activities. This book is like anything else in life, the more you put into it the more you will get out of it! Enjoy! The more you allow yourself to discover the truth within, the greater the benefit.

"Body Awareness and Reflection" section is included in the first chapter. Let yourself become aware of a variety of experiences in your body, mind, emotions, spirit and soul with dance. Be aware of emotional releases and thoughts, insights, painful or traumatic experiences. You can explore and reflect upon your physical experiences with your body and movement after reading each chapter.

Dance with the topic of each chapter. Let your body move to your own inner rhythms and to music that you enjoy and inspires you. The questions at the end of the chapter are for your reflection to gain insights for growth and healing.

Dancing with your story from the inside out is an opportunity to be honest and find the story deep within you. You can make a conscious choice to know the truth within. Let the truth of your story heal and set you free.

1

What Is a Story?

Stories can hide the truth. Stories can seek the truth

Dictionary.com defines *story* as "a narrative, either true or fictitious, in prose or verse, designed to inter, amuse, or instruct the listener, or reader; a tale. A story can include fictitious, tales, shorter and less elaborate than a novel such as a branch of literature, the plot or succession of incidents of a novel, poem, drama, etc. The characterizations were good but the story was weak. Narration of an incident or a series of events or an example of these that is or may be narrated, as an anecdote, joke etc. A narration of the events in the life of a person or the existence of a thing, or such events as a subject for narration: The story of medicine; the story of his life; a report or account of a matter, a statement or allegation." *Miriam-webster.com* defines *story* as "an account of incidents or events; a statement regarding the facts pertinent to a situation in question."

Stories are born and come alive in family legacies, conversations, folklores, fairytales, true stories, fictional stories, books, dances, novels, myths, movies, visual art, photographs, and theater. Cultural stories help individuals define leadership, love, men, women, music, dance, singing, and silence. Cultural stories place an imprint of the expectations of who we are in our lives. Theater and movies reveal the vision of human life through time, sound, and space. It offers flesh and blood of human beings involved in human action. We must remind ourselves to not get lost in the tragedy, comedy, and dramatic experiences. Our experiences communicate an insight, message, or reflection about us or the human condition. Theaters, like novels, tell us a story—are make-believe. Through gesture or movement, language, character ideas, and spectacle, it imitates in living form. Theater, movies, books, and music are intricate, creative "life scenes" that we respond to in body, mind, and spirit. Like theater, cinema confronts us with life similarly found on our streets, but without the live performers. Through the magic and sophistication of technology and special effects, new worlds open for us like no other art form. Our response and identification with the characters, plot, theme and message pulls us in. And, as a result, what we are watching, reading or hearing becomes real and alive. Art stimulates our senses; it touches our heart and soul. Artistic expression involves us in its product in many ways, emotionally or intellectually. It creates an interest that tantalizes and stimulates us. Our human ancestors drew pictures in caves to tell stories. Dance has been an important part of human culture, rituals and ceremony to celebrate, honor and entertain, since the birth of the earliest human civilizations. Indigenous people dance to celebrate, rejoice, and bury the dead. Dance is a method of healing and expression. We are born to move and dance.

Storytelling Is the Oldest Healing Art in the World

Stories and the art of storytelling have been in existence since the beginning of humankind. Storytelling is the oldest healing art in the world. We enjoy listening, watching, and learning the stories from our ancestors, as well as from current art, entertainment, news, media, books, and music. As human beings, we are natural storytellers. Our stories are based on facts or completely made-up. As a culture we have great true stories: *Catch Me If You Can, 12 Years a Slave, American Hustle, Steve Jobs, Selma, Heaven Is for Real, and Everest.* Art, books, movies, theater, music, photographs, and, most of all, people tell stories.

An example of a great story is Joseph Campbell's, Hero's Journey, a *monomyth* or a story or narrative that is found around the world.

In this story, the hero begins in the ordinary world and receives a calling to enter an unknown world of extraordinary powers and events. The hero accepts this call, enters an unfamiliar world, to face tasks, trials, and tribulations, either alone or with someone else. The requirement is that the hero must survive a severe challenge. If the hero survives, the hero accomplishes a prodigious gift. The hero decides whether to stay or return to the ordinary world, where he or she faces challenges on the return journey. If the journey is successful, the hero uses the gift to improve the world. The stories of Osiris, Prometheus, Moses, and Buddha, Batman, Superman, Queen Elizabeth, Helen of Troy, Jeanne of Arc, Aphrodite, Cleopatra, and Nefertiti follow the heroes' and heroines' journey.

As you can tell, the hero's story draws you right into it. You become the hero and the character you are reading about, whether it is real or not. It becomes real in the moment that you read it, just like watching a good movie or diving into a good book. The story appeals to your senses, body, emotions, thoughts, intellect, heart, and soul. You are all in the story. This can be a metaphor for our personal stories as a hero or a heroine. Are you the hero in your own story?

Indigenous people dance to celebrate, inspire the elements and nature, rejoice, and bury the dead. They believe that when you are disheartened, you need to ask yourself the questions: Did you stop dancing? Did you stop singing? When in your life did you stop being enchanted by stories, particularly your own life story? Did you stop listening to the sweet territory of silence? The human condition exists just as we are conditioned to eat, cry, and laugh, we are designed to move and dance. Stories live in our head and dance is in our body. We all have an original imprint, and we all have a story to tell. We live, believe, enjoy, delight, lead, and feel the impact of our stories. Stories of pain and negative experiences lead us to cry and lose ourselves and can stop our dance. What is the music of pain? Can you dance through your painful stories? Some stories we like and others, we dislike. We get to choose which ones we want to tell and share and which ones we keep secret.

My fascination with stories began as a child. I loved listening to people, especially elderly people. As a young girl, I slept with my grandmother when she visited our home. I enjoyed listening to my grandmother tell me stories from the Ann Landers column in the newspaper. Now I know why I received a degree in psychology and counseling. I became a professional listener for my client's and their stories. As a teenager, I took four busses to a private all-girl high school. Every day, an elderly black woman and I would sit together on the bus. I would listen to everything that she told me with fascination. I was intrigued by her stories and with what she shared with me. She told me that when I became forty years old, I would be a very wise woman. During college, I loved the stories of mythology, especially Aphrodite being born of the sea and the myth of Cupid and Psyche. I am a lover of stories in books, movies, theater, song, dance, music, and whatever medium I can find! I loved dancing as early as I can remember and was voted the "best dancer" of my high school. I love the marriage of music and dance. Dance has helped me to adjust to different living situations in my life. When I moved to Maui, learning to dance Hawaiian Hula helped me to integrate living in the Hawaiian culture.

Creating Your Story

Life happens, and so do stories. Everyone has a story to tell. Everyone has their own life story. The story we tell ourselves is our best story. This book delights in storytelling and discerns between empowering and disheartening stories.

Life events happen naturally, such as divorce, death, career, graduation, marriage, promotion, adoption, abandonment, ill health, and abuse. Know that everything that happens is an opportunity to grow and evolve. The painful response to life events are growing pains for the highest good, even though they do not feel very good. These growing pains move in a way that we need to know and learn. Growing pains in the physical sense can be painful. It is like starting a new exercise program; when you first begin to move and stretch muscles that have not been exercised in a while, it can be painful. Moving forward on a physical, emotional, mental, and spiritual level can also be uncomfortable. Just remember, it is only pain. You can handle it. Life is a great teacher. When we let life have all of us, we gain through the pain.

Why Do You Create Stories?

As human beings, we not only live in the world of stories, but we are always creating and telling stories. A life experience is painful, and as the pain begins to grow, so does the story we create about it. The stages of pain trigger and stimulate thoughts, feelings, and emotions. We have the ability to put this together and create a story about it. We know pain doesn't feel very good and that there are many levels of pain. We also know that as human beings, we experience pain and suffering, even though we try to avoid it. Pain can stop our dance and stunt our growth, if we let it. When we realize that pain is an opportunity for healing and growth, we can be okay with it. So do you think we create stories about life events to create or avoid pain? How do you think that works? Do we feel better if we create a story or blame someone else for our pain? We know we can choose to rewrite and let go of our stories.

Human beings often engage in irrational behavior. In other words, behavior that doesn't necessarily make sense. We can be vindictive and petty and rationalize, project behavior, and basically ignore the facts and the truth. We can deceive ourselves in many ways. Human ego-centrism and self-centeredness are natural human tendencies. The human ego regards itself as the center of its world. Everything else has little or no regard, including other peoples' interests, attitudes, beliefs, needs, and wants other than our own. If human nature is to be egocentric and self-serving, then the stories we create also center around and serve the self. We create stories for many reasons. We get something from our stories and the sharing of them. Most people love to talk about themselves. When people share their stories, they are talking about themselves or at least, in part. When a life event happens to us and we tell it to others, we are storytelling our version and interpretation of what happened. Sometimes we add a few extras, such as our feelings, perception, perspectives, and give it a flavor to make it our own. In other words, we give it our signature. If and when we get honest with ourselves, we become aware of what we are doing in sharing our story.

You may ask, why would we want to do this? The answer is: for a variety of reasons, motives, and agendas. This can include feeling better, looking good, and serving our self in some way, shape, or form. The bottom line is we get something by doing what we do. Sharing our stories serve us in some way. Being honest allows us to see what we get and the ways our stories serve us.

Whether our stories are real or made-up, consciously or unconsciously, they serve the *self*. The *self* is who we are to ourselves. When we look at who we are from within, we come from the *self*. When we are alone, we are being with the part of who we are called the *self*. When we look at who we are to others, we are coming from our *person*. When we are being with others and socializing, we are in the part of ourselves called our *person*. When we drop out of our "self" and our "person," we are in our heart. Our heart is the entrance into "being."

When Do You Create a Story?

Stories are created when we talk about a life event and come from our "self." Our event is interpreted and communicated in the form of a story. We create a story when we change the way it really happened. We add our own details and meaning. Creating a story is similar to being a bystander or a witness for an accident or incident involving other people. When we retell the event, we add or subtract something about the event that happened. Most eyewitness bystander's testimonies are not substantial for this reason. These bystander testimonies may not be accepted as evidence also because of selective memory and forgetfulness.

How Does a Life Event Become a Story?

Each individual perceives an event in their own way. Our story is our perception and interpretation of an event. Our view is the way we see it and share it with others. Both of these elements generate a story from our perspective. Our understanding adds to the individually distinct flavor of a story. Each story is different and delivered by the individual, who experienced the event and created the story about it. Each person adds their unique flavors, culture, experiences, family history, patterns, likes, dislikes, and a variety of other sources. Are your stories enchanting with originality and character?

You Can Change and Alter a Story by Knowing You Created It

Life happens. Life comes at us in many forms such as an event, situation, issue, pattern, or circumstance. Everyone has their own perception of the event. We are unique, and our perceptions and interpretations of events may differ. When meaning is given to the story, it makes the story bigger as it grows along. Relating and believing a story can make it seem real. We integrate it into our lives, and then, our life becomes our story.

- *Event*
    Life happens, for instance, when someone gets a divorce. This is a good example, because it involves two people. There are always two sides to a story! Each person has their own perception, experiences, interpretation, feelings, emotions, thoughts, occurrences, and understanding of the event. Each person has their own view and perspective of what happened. This is a generic example as a reference.

- *Perception*
    The husband says that his wife did not give him enough sex so he was justified in having an affair. The wife says that she was sick and ill and unable to satisfy her husband's and

her own sexual needs. Both have a different perception of the same event which is separation and divorce.

- *Interpretation*

    Both interpret the divorce situation in their own way. They interpret the reason for the divorce according to their own frame of reference.

- *Meaning*

    We add our personal meaning to it from our interpretation of the event. Each person gives it their own meaning. In the above example, the husband may make it mean that women don't satisfy men's sexual needs in sex. The wife may make it mean that all men want is sex and they have affairs if they don't get what they want.

- *Beliefs*

    Believing our story to be true, whether it is or is not, impacts us on many levels. Beliefs can shape who we think we are, what we become and mold into our lives.

Relatedness to a Story

Relatedness is our resonance with the story. Our story is relative and real. Yes, the facts may be real, but our story about the facts may be made–up, and we believe what we made up. For example, if a person with a challenging past of abusive parents or has addictive parents, divorced parents, is dealing with the death of a parent, was adopted or in foster care, they may relate to their story as part of their identity. They may see themselves in their story and their story in themselves. They may make what happened to them affect their self-image, self-esteem, and worth. They may not value themselves, because of the story they relate to about what happened to them as a child.

You can easily get caught in the trap of identifying with your story. You may even lose yourself in the process. The truth is you are not your experiences or your story. The real you is much bigger than a story. There is a value in distinguishing between a life event and the meaning we give it. Knowing the difference between the two is important. Your life experiences are not who you are, and neither is your story. Know that they are two completely different things. Realizing the golden nuggets in life experiences helps us to distinguish between the two and integrate the lessons learned from them. Receive the gifts and gain the insights, from life experiences as you evolve and begin a journey of personal growth, health and well-being.

Everyone has life lessons, whether they are aware of them or not. One of my favorite sayings is "Just because you do not see something does not mean it does not exist!" You can look at life as one big school. We all have lessons to learn, and sometimes, these may be difficult and challenging lessons. Realize that you are not the lessons, experiences, challenges, or difficulties. Sometimes it may be difficult to separate you from your experience, but know that you are not your experience or your story. If you are caught up in your story by sharing it with others and thinking about it a lot, take note of it. Talking about your story reinforces it as true, making it bigger and stronger. You feed it with your attention and energy. Be aware that you are not your story or your past. You are a being with a past and experiences.

I once told my philosophy teacher that I was an artist. He replied, "You are not an artist, you are a being that enjoys doing art."

Belief and Response

Beliefs about an event from the past may or may not be true. But each person believes their story for the truth. When an individual is moving in clarity, they are clear in their knowing and seeing a situation. The question is: Are we being honest? Are we being honest about what happened? Or, did we make up some part so the situation up? Sometimes stories are true and sometimes false. It depends on the awareness, clarity and honesty of the individual.

Beliefs affect individuals on a physical, mental, emotional, and spiritual level. The truth is the event happened and it was painful. Accept the event and your lessons as part of your life journey, history, and past.

Detachment

Can you leave it in your past and not bring it with you? Detachment is an aspect of distinguishing between an event, story, and *you*. Know that you are not your story or your past. Begin to know what it feels like to discern the difference between what happened to you and *you*. Attachment to our stories can makes it difficult to detach from them. They become integrated into who we think we are that we can't distinguish the difference. Being stuck in our past or a story can challenge personal growth. You may be in a new relationship, but at the same time, find yourself being reminded of the thoughts and feelings from a previous partner. Letting go of the story, and moving past the past, can help you move forward in your new relationship. I have listened to my favorite music that moved my body and inspired me. Dance and music helped me to let go and move forward. How can you allow music and dance to help you to let go and move forward?

For years, I struggled with the fact of losing my parents at a young age and learning to live without them. I watched other families with children enjoying a vacation and being together, laughing and having a good time. I wished I was a child in that family. I would envy other friends with parents to talk to, lean on at difficult times and share daily events. It took me years of counseling, psychology, and inner child therapy to heal and detach from my past. I knew I needed help on both mental, and emotional levels. For this reason, I became a guidance counselor, therapist, and provisional psychologist to learn new ways to be healthy.

I completed my education and several degrees to heal myself and others in the process. My story about my divorce shifted when I released my feeling of guilt and realized I was not responsible for his feelings and pain. I know that I am not responsible for the reactions, responses, thoughts and feelings of others. I finally realized that my experiences, past, tragedies, and events are not who I am. I am not my past, tragedies, and experiences. I am a loving human being who has experienced this past and these events.

Life

We get to choose to live our lives being our stories and living from them. Or, letting go, growing, and transforming in the beautiful being that we truly are! We get to choose. Are you ready to begin that journey?

Dancing with Your Story from the Inside Out

The purpose of this exercise is to go inside yourself, realize your story, dance, move your body, and let go. Don't forget to breathe! Enjoy being in the moment, relaxing and releasing and not thinking about what the steps or how you look. Be free to just be you with the music and dance!

Dance

Put your favorite music on, take deep breaths, relax, and let your body move you. Do not think about steps or what you look like. Dance as if no one is watching you! Enjoy being creative and alive!

- Did physical sensations become present in your body?
- What are your thoughts, feelings, emotions, story, issue, or life experience?
- Write your responses in your personal journal.
- Dance with each chapter title in this book. Put the music on that moves you, and let your body speak to you through dance!
- Write and reflect about your dance and experiences.

Body Awareness and Reflection

Know that all of your experiences and life stories are stored deep within the cells of your body.

- Be aware and present to your physicality.
- How are you feeling? Do you feel good? Do you feel aches and pains? If so, where do you feel in pain?

- When you think about your story/stories and how does your body feel and respond to it?
- What messages did your body tell you about your story?

In the beginning, you may not be aware of any. Be patient. Be open to being sensitive and aware of any subtle changes or feelings or thoughts. Apply body awareness and reflection to each chapter.

Writing and Dance Reflection

- What does beginning this journey mean to you?

  _____

  _____

- What do I want to accomplish in reading and doing the activities?

  _____

  _____

- What are my goals?

  _____

  _____

- What specific stories would I like to let go of?

  _____

  _____

Dance Reflection.

Dance and let your body move to your own inner rhythms. Let your body take you into the dance. Where is the dance in your story? Where is the story in your dance? Write down your dance experiences.

  _____

  _____

2

Seeing Through Your Own Lens

Stories Are in the Eyes of the Beholder

Ernest Hemingway was once challenged to write a complete short story in only six words, a literary legend says. He came back with a brilliant six-word story and won the bet. Annie Horowitz, a fabulous photographer, lets us see life through the lens of her beautiful photography.

Living through a lens is seeing life through the click of our own camera. As most things in life, there is a positive and negative side to everything. We can look at living through our lens as having a good aspect and a not-so-good aspect. Unfortunately, interruptions alter our focus and vision. This means, the lens can be cluttered or fogged up with our experiences and with egocentricity (being the center of our world) and self-bias (bias to a self-serving view). How do we clean it up to allow ourselves to clearly see through the lens? It begins with the awareness that we are seeing through a personal perspective. It is so familiar, as our natural way of seeing that we miss it! Our filters and boundaries interfere with our clarity in the way we see ourselves and our life. The way we see things is influenced by the conscious and subconscious aspects of the self. The subconscious is as much a part of the self as the conscious self. The subconscious self has the greater impact and the conscious aspect represents the smaller part of the self. Most of our experiences are determined by the foundation of the subconscious self. Have you ever wondered why you can revisit the same experience/event and see it differently? This way of seeing becomes our "norm." It is normal for us to experience ourselves through this lens.

A door opens the moment we realize there is a new way of seeing. We can have a status quo, stay stuck, or change. We know there is a different way. When we really get that we have been living our entire life from stories, we shift. This shift opens a new space in how we see ourselves and past events. We no longer have to live our lives according to our story. We set ourselves free.

Here is a simple example; a child in third grade does not do well in math. In high school, she fails all of her math courses. As an adult, she does not balance her personal accounts. Throughout her life, she continues to have problems with anything math-related She only uses the calculator for anything in her life that involves math, such as addition, subtraction, division, and multiplication. She fails her college preliminary math classes. She experiences the self-fulfilling prophecy, which is what she believes about herself, the story that she does not do well in math. Therefore it happens and manifests in her life.

The awareness and realization of creating a story—in this case, a dislike for math—is the first step in changing it. This opens a new door of change. The door sets us free from the tightness, drama, and familiarity of our story. It can open whenever we want it to. All we need to do is to know that it is there and we are free to go through it. We are then able to free ourselves of a story and/or have no story at all.

This freedom lets us live from who we really are, which is not about having a story, it is about being. Being means to just be and not do. Try being with another person, a loved one, friend or a tree. Enjoy being in the present moment with another individual or with nature. Nature compliments us, because nature knows who we really are. Nature sees us just as we are in that moment. We do not need to change anything about ourselves or do anything different, and we do not need to tell nature our stories! But if you want to, that is okay too. Nature hears and listens to us. Nature is a great teacher in learning how to just be.

How Does Our Life Become Our Story?

If a situation in a family, such as the death of a loved one, happens, will it be interpreted in the same way? Life happens, and, yes, we see it through our own lens. Our response to an event is so automatic and unconscious. We are not even aware that we are doing it. The world we live in becomes the story of our reality. Each person sees and interprets life events in different ways.

The purpose of this book is to disconnect the automatic and unconscious response of thoughts and feelings to life events. An invitation to take the time to be honest and discern the facts from the story. We begin to see something new. You may look at someone and say, "Why do they keep doing the same thing over and over again? Don't they get it? Can't they see what they are doing?" As mentioned earlier, it is easier to see someone else's behavior than our own. We are so used to seeing life our way. We forget there may be other ways of perceiving and being in life. Whatever our thoughts, feelings, actions and behavior may be, it automatically becomes our normal way of being. This is our norm. We may have a knee-jerk reaction to ourselves and how we live our life until we follow what we know the truth of and challenge something new and different.

How Do We Make Our Story Real?

A life event is a life event. Perceptions, meaning and opinions, create a story. The story about a life event, we accept as being true. We believe it is real. Framing our life events makes stories out of them. We can make books, music, songs and write music about stories but it still doesn't make them real. All stories have a combination of truth and facts. Stories serve a purpose, our purpose. Remember that human beings are naturally egocentric.

Our world revolves around our ego and self. We may not even realize or be aware of it. So if that is true, why do we create stories from our real-life events? The answer is: our stories serve us in some way. We are the only ones that know how they serve us. Honesty can help us answer this question. Honesty guides us to know and see the truth in the life event, our stories, interpretations and beliefs.

Here's how it works, when a life event happens, we perceive, interpret, and give it meaning. We create a story about it, and then we *believe* that story. We physically, mentally, emotionally, and spiritually respond to the story. We live our life according to the story. We make the story real. Framing a life event as a story is very powerful, because once we realize that we created a story, we can change it. We transform and empower ourselves by the truth of what we know. We transform as we focus time and energy on what is real and grow into healthy human beings in the process.

This chapter focuses on how life events become our story and how we live from them. We will learn to transform by knowing that our stories are not real and not who we are. We can be a new and different person in the process of untelling our story and empowered without the identification of our story. Now that we know we create our stories, let's experience how. We all experience love, rejection, abandonment, disappointment, betrayal, joy, happiness, elation, excitement, depression, and suffering. We create stories about these circumstances in our lives.

In chapter one, we discussed the reasons we create stories. But now I am going to add another reason to the list. We create stories to make excuses, to not be responsible, to offer reasons, to procrastinate, to explain, and to justify our actions and behavior. These are our causes our *be*-causes. In psychology, Freud refers to this aspect of behavior as our defense mechanisms, another way we protect and defend ourselves is with our stories.

A few years ago, I hired a book agent for an inspirational book about dance, women, and the journey of the feminine spirit. I was so excited when I found out that she was a Hay House Publishing book representative. I waited and waited to hear from her after she sent my book to this publishing company. Finally, I decided to call her, even though I was nervous about what I was about to find out about my book. Her husband answered the phone and told me that none of the authors were accepted by this publisher. I asked how many authors' book proposals were sent. He told me several other authors' books were sent. I was disappointed not only because my book was not accepted by this desired publishing company, but that the agent represented several other authors. I thought I was the only book outline being presented. When I asked the book agent if any author she represented was accepted by this publishing company, she replied with a big NO. I felt disappointed, depressed, unmotivated and defeated about ever becoming a successful author with a traditional publishing company. I rewrote my story about this event, because here you are reading my book!

Now that we know we create our stories, let's experience how.

- *Life Event*
  Life events can be any event in your life a situation or a circumstance a happening to you or others around you
  What is a real life event that happened to you?

- *Perceive*
  Perception is the way we see, recognize, and observe the life event.
  What do you see? How did you view this life event?

- *Emotional Reaction*
  Emotions play an important role in our response to a life event. Our emotions, such as love, anger, jealousy, fear, etc., give away our feelings to a particular situation. The way we feel about a situation can interfere with the way we see it. This interference can distort our view and the truth about the event.
  How do you comprehend the life event?

- *Interpret*
  Interpretation is the construction, deductive reasoning, and understanding of the life event.

31

How did you relate to the life event as it occurred? What is your understanding of the life event?

- *Meaning*

  Meaning is the significance and importance given to the life event.

  What did you make it mean? What does it signify to you? What did this life event point out to you?

We all have filters that we see our life through. For example, we may have a rose-, blue-, or gray-colored lens. Our filters are colored with our thoughts, feelings, emotions, personal history, the past, our culture, history, beliefs, values, and experiences. They influence the ways in which we perceive our world. We all perceive our life in distinct and exceptional ways. The question is, have you ever noticed how easy it is to see someone else's dilemma, issues, stories, past, etc.? When we view a situation or event from our own frame of reference and our own eyes, our filters get in the way of truly seeing it from an objective viewpoint.

Seeing through our filters and boundaries can be either subjective or objective. Looking through our own lens can be challenging and difficult to see the truth of a situation. How can we overcome this dilemma and let ourselves really see the truth of a situation? We can be honest and allow ourselves to see the truth of what we know about a particular situation or life event.

Past Experiences

Leave the past behind, so the future can move forward! Our past experiences can also influence our story of a life event. Past experiences can be a filter in how we perceive it. Challenges can occur with the element of previously experienced thoughts and feelings around an event. For example, a person who gets a divorce and then remarries can experience the same issue, as in spousal infidelity and another divorce. It can be challenging discerning the thoughts and feelings left over from the unhealed wounds of the first divorce or from the current divorce experience. We begin to cloud our view and our vision by what is happening again and what we are reliving. How do we discern our old stories from the new ones? Discernment comes with knowing, honesty, and awareness. Making this distinction is an important one. Look to see if you are recreating the same or similar life event in your life over and over again.

Here is a suggestion. Sit down with a pen and paper. Research states that the most powerful writing communication comes from the physical hand on the paper, which has the greatest impact on the mind and body connection.

The act of writing accesses your left brain, which is analytical and rational. While your left brain is occupied, your right brain is free to create, intuit and feel. In sum, writing removes mental blocks and allows you to use all of your brainpower to better understand yourself, others, and the world around you.

Journaling health benefits are to:

- *Clarify your thoughts and feelings.* Do you ever seem all jumbled up inside, unsure of what you want or feel? Taking a few minutes to jot down your thoughts and emotions (no editing!) will quickly get you in touch with your internal world.

- *Know yourself better.* By writing routinely, you will get to know what makes you feel happy and confident. You will also become clear about situations and people who are toxic for you, as well as important information for your emotional well-being.

- *Reduce stress.* Writing about anger, sadness, and other painful emotions helps to release the intensity of these feelings. By doing so, you will feel calmer and better able to stay in the present.

- *Solve problems more effectively.* Typically, we problem solve from a left-brained, analytical perspective. But sometimes the answer can only be found by engaging right-brained creativity and intuition. Writing unlocks these other capabilities, and affords the opportunity for unexpected solutions to seemingly unsolvable problems.

- *Resolve disagreements with others.* Writing about misunderstandings, rather than being upset over them, will help you to understand another's point of view. And you may also come up with a sensible resolution to the conflict.

Keeping a journal allows you to track patterns, trends, improvement, and personal growth over time. When current circumstances appear insurmountable, you will be able to look back confidently on previous dilemmas that you have since resolved.

Story as an Identity

We can identify and define ourselves through our story. For instance, we all have a story to tell about ourselves and our lives. What do you enjoy talking about when you are at a social event? Having a story and sharing a story is okay. What you are being invited to look at is taking the story out of context and making it bigger than it really is. Or, we can make a story mean something that it doesn't mean or we think it means, because it happened to us. The less emotionally or mentally reactive we are to a life event, the more we can know and see the truth in it.

Seeing through a New Lens

You have an opportunity to see your situation/story in a different way. Would someone else see your situation differently? Would they be able to see it more objectively? When you remove yourself from the event, you can see the story you created objectively. I have done this several times in my life. I have stepped away to be able to see a clearer picture. You gain insight and a new vision! Now, you can rethink the situation from a new place.

It is like looking at the mountain. When we are too close to a situation or circumstance in our lives, our vision and our reality become distorted, because we are too close. Stepping farther away from a mountain allows you to have a different view. It is good to take a step back. Perhaps remove your thoughts and feelings about a situation for a while and then revisit it. Looking with refreshed eyes creates a new way of seeing. We can dance, write in a journal, talk to a friend, and join a support or discussion group, either online or in a blog or draw a picture.

Write your FACTS and STORY here:

FACTS   STORY

Write the details (What is your story about the event?)

EXAMPLES OF FACTS AND STORY

FACTS

A woman gets married and goes on a honeymoon.

STORY

This woman did not enjoy the place she visited on her honeymoon. She shares her disappointment and feelings with her friends. She states that she will never return to this tropical island.

FACTS

A student fails an English course in college.

STORY

The student shares with classmates that she dislikes this college. She tells others she is not a good student.

FACTS

A wife leaves her husband for another man. The marriage ends in divorce.

STORY

The husband's story is: I will never get married again. I was married once, and my wife left me. Marriage does not work for me.

Writing and Dance Reflection

Discovering your story!

_____

_____

Be honest with yourself in this exercise!

_____

_____

Write down the happening and occurrence of the life event
(What are the details?)

_____

_____

What are your perceptions about the situation?
(How do you see the situation?)

_____

_____

What is your interpretation of the situation?
(What is your understanding of the situation?)

_____

_____

What is your opinion about what happened?
(Do you agree or disagree or like or dislike the
situation?)

_____

_____

What are your thoughts?
(When you think about the situation, what comes to your
mind?)

_____

_____

What are your feelings?
(What feelings are experienced when you think about the situation?)

_____

_____

What emotions are you experiencing as a result of this life event?
Name the emotions such as happiness, anger, sadness, joy, elation, disappointment.

_____

_____

Describe the ways this life experience triggers you.
(Can you think of a past situation or circumstance similar to this one?)
(Is it the same pattern repeating over and over again?)

_____

_____

Dance Reflection

Dance and reflect by allowing yourself to dance with the facts and with the story. Dance is unique movement through time and space. Put your favorite music on and let your body move to it. Write down what you observe in your dance.

_____

_____

_____

_____

3

How Does Your Life Reflect Your Story?

Stories mirror and reflect the way we see ourselves

When you look in the mirror what do you see? Do you think others see you in the same way? Stories can be a mirror for you to view yourself. Mirrors reflect you from your own eyes. You can create a story about your mirror reflection and believe it. Whether your stories about your mirror reflection are positive or negative views, they can be a hindrance. Either reflection can hinder you from seeing the truth about you in the mirror. You may see yourself in the way others tell you are. In order to know the truth you have to be honest with yourself and trust your knowing.

There was a time in my life that I avoided looking in the mirror. When I would look at pictures of myself, I would tell myself that couldn't be me. I am not that overweight. But the truth was that I was overweight and not being truthful with myself. I was avoiding the truth about myself. The story I created about my being overweight was untrue and I was unable to face the truth. It was not until several years later, that I focused on a new style of eating, that the weight dropped off. As long as I was telling myself that story, I was not going to lose the weight because I was in denial about it. The lesson here is to be aware of what you tell yourself and others.

Discover the way you use stories. When life happens, your reaction to the event can impact and determine the way you see yourself. If you are happy about an event, you may feel empowered and good. If a negative happening occurs, you may react by negative feelings and be upset.

Take for example, your parents got divorced, and you felt sad and upset. You felt abandoned. Abandonment feelings can have a strong impact on the way you think and feel about yourself. Abandonment feelings can trigger thoughts and beliefs about being unworthy of love, or a fear about opening your heart to love. The way you interpret the divorce and your emotional reaction can reflect into your self-concept, value and self-worth. You can turn these negative feelings inward and begin to feel bad and do not understand why. You create a story about your parents' divorce without even realizing it. Children often place themselves in the middle of their parents' divorce and feel responsible for it. And, these feeling get integrated into how they feel about themselves.

Life experiences, events and our stories about them can mirror the way we see ourselves. Know that you are not your experiences or your stories. Remember, life is always happening. An open and soft heart is most important in the way we respond. Feelings are just feelings, and your thoughts are just thoughts. Neither your feelings, thoughts or your stories can define you, only if you let them.

How Does Our Life Reflect Our Story?

Events become stories about weddings, births, and deaths. An event is just an event until we either create a story about it or identify with it. Our life reflects our story through our identification with it. We identify ourselves through the eyes of our story. We are in all of our stories whether we are aware of it or not. When we do this, we let our story become a part of us. We invite our stories into our lives and our lives into our stories. These stories are now integrated into who we are. When we view ourselves through the eyes of our story, we begin to live our life from that framework.

A story is just a story until we give it the power to become more than just a story. A story is how we talk about our life experiences and events. We are not victims of our stories. Stories can become part of how we see ourselves, our self-concept, self-esteem, and self-image. When our stories are part of our self as a social construct in the way we perceive ourselves, it is reflected in relation to how we perceive others. Our perceptions include not only seeing ourselves in others, but seeing others in ourselves. What is important to know is that our stories can be an unconscious act. Take this opportunity to be real and truthful with yourself. Allow yourself to see the stories that are in your life. And, identify which ones are hindering your evolution and growth.

"I am not good at dating," says Jerry. "I know I would rather stay home instead of doing the dating scene again. Most people I meet are not interested in having a real relationship. I don't think I look good enough to be dating. But I am going back out into the dating world, and I want to look good. So I signed up at the gym".

Jerry believes he is not good at dating. His belief is that most people aren't available or interested in a real relationship. He created this story as a result of being rejected several times. Jerry doesn't think he looks good enough to be dating. His solution is joining the gym to look and feel better. This is Jerry's story. He believes his story to be true, whether it is or not.

Story Journal

- How can you relate to Jerry's story, his beliefs about himself, and how it shows up in his life?

- What is a situation you are experiencing now in your life?

- What do you feel or think about yourself in this situation?

- How does your identity show up in your story?

- What are your beliefs about it?

- How does it show up in your life?

Our identity can reflect our story in ways that we may or may not realize. We can begin to define ourselves as who we are through the lens of our story. Again, we are not talking about truth here. We are talking about our story about what is true.

Jose, is a young man in his twenties, who had a horrific past and childhood. Both parents were drug addicts. His father was given a life sentence of imprisonment. His mother gave him to her parents to raise at 8 years old.

At nine years old, his grandparents gave him up for adoption. His adoptive parents gave him a good education and did everything they could to help him in a positive way. At eighteen, he choose not to go to the prepaid college. He wanted to be his "own"person and make his career choices. How will Jose' childhood impact the way he sees himself and his life? Do you think Jose will live from his story about his childhood? Or, will Jose be able to create a new future, and and be free of his story?

When living through a story lens, we give meaning to the story and then we believe it. We can be conscious or unconscious of this happening. Beliefs are derived from the meaning of our stories. This impacts how we think and feel about ourselves which reflects in our way of being in life. The view of ourselves reflects our way of being in the world.

As a guidance counselor working with children of divorce, I learned that they blame themselves for their parents' problems. They feel responsible for their parents' divorce. Group interventions were discussed to explain to children that they were not the reason for their parents' divorce. Their parents' parted ways because of their own reasons.

Rejection is an emotional response that can be experienced when someone we love leaves or ends a relationship. We may create a story about ourselves based upon these feelings. The pain of being rejected engenders deep feelings of inadequacy and self-hatred. This in turn can cause anger toward ourselves and others. Jose may endure a negative sense of self from his painful past or he may not. If he blames himself or identifies with his past, it may interfere with his identity and the way he sees himself.

The most critical wounds of abandonment, shame, and betrayal, occur when they are internalized and integrated in a personal way. Without recovery, this wound can leave a scar that hides deep beneath the surface, as it continues to generate insecurity and undermine self-esteem for decades. In the process of grieving the loss of someone's love, we experience abandonment and begin to doubt our own self-worth.

Our story begins when we reflect upon what happened to us, our thoughts, and our feelings. We begin to identify with the event by internalizing shameful thoughts and feelings. Shame appears when we believe there is something wrong with us. A betrayal of trust appears when someone we love is unfaithful in fulfilling a promise or vow. We weave our reactions, thoughts, and feelings into the way we see and feel about ourselves. This becomes the foundation for our self-image, worth, and value.

Challenges occur when we realize that we do this every time we think, feel, or tell our story. Our beliefs are an internal reflection of our story. The more emphasis we give to our beliefs being true, the more powerful and real they become. Our stories about abandonment or wealth are not who we are. It does not matter if events are positive or negative, good or bad, they are not our identity. Whether we drive a Rolls Royce or ride a bicycle to work, the experience does not define who we are.

Story, Self-Image, Self-Concept, and Self-Esteem

Self-image refers to how we imagine others perceive us. When we identify our self-image with our story, what do you think happens? Do we see clearly through the lens of our story? Sometimes it may be difficult to not identify with our story. If we look closely, there may be some residue of our story that reflects how we think others see us or how we see ourselves. *Self-concept* is the idea or mental image an individual has of oneself and one's strengths, weaknesses, status, etc. *Self-esteem* is a favorable impression we give to ourselves.

The way we view ourselves is based upon a social construct; it is how we perceive ourselves in relation to how we perceive others. If we admire someone for their intelligence, talents, beauty, sex appeal, strength, or abilities, we may judge our self-esteem in this social context. The way we see ourselves can easily be distorted not only because of our stories, but also because of our lack of ability to see objectively. When we look at ourselves, we see ourselves through subjective eyes. We can be objective in the way we see others, but looking at ourselves is subjective. This means, our view belongs to the thinking subject instead of the object of thought as in being objective.

Comparing Stories

Is my story better or worse than yours? A comparison to others is a moot point! Know that you are the only one like you in the world. You are one of a kind, and there is no one else like you. Everyone has a unique fingerprint as well as a unique eye image. The gifts you offer to the world belong to only you. Sometimes we can even use our stories to compare ourselves to others. Comparing stories to others' stories can impact and influence the way we see and feel about ourselves. We may feel better or less than others as we compare ourselves to them. In other words, we can inflate our egos or deflate them as we relate and see our reflection.

For years growing up as a child and young adult after losing my parents from illness, I would compare myself to friends and family members who had parents. My story was that I felt cheated and sad that my parents passed away at a young age, and I did not have them to share my life with as I became an adult. I was constantly comparing and dreaming that what if my parents were alive again. What would my life look like? How would I be different?

Here are some suggestions to rewrite your story and recreate your self-image, self-concept, and self-esteem. Regardless of your story about yourself and your life, you can transform your story by listening to what you honestly know about yourself. Take a look at all of your accomplishments and achievements. Whether large or small, how do these accomplishments and achievements impact the way you see yourself? Through this process, you will learn to love yourself first.

At the heart of every story is the truth.

When you realize that you are the one who created the stories and beliefs about yourself and your life, you set yourself. Know that an event is an event no matter how horrific the occurrence. The situations, circumstances, issues, and problems in your life are an opportunity to grow, evolve, and become a better person. Whatever happened to you does not make you any less of a person; it is just what happened. Be okay with it! When we take a moment to look at the meaning that we give it, we begin to realize that it is all made-up! Take a moment to write about the freedom that you are experiencing from your story.

Writing and Dance Reflection

- What is an accomplishment that you are most proud of?

  _____

  _____

- What were you patted on the back and acknowledged for by your friends, family, workplace, community?

  _____

  _____

- What do your friends tell you they like about you the most?

  _____

  _____

- What is your greatest gift?

  _____

  _____

- What do you admire most in yourself?

  _____

  _____

- Do your friend's assessments of you match your own?

  _____

  _____

- What additional talents, gifts, abilities and assets would you like to recognize?

  _____

  _____

- In what ways does the story of your life impact your self-image, self-concept and self-esteem?

  _____

  _____

- How does this view of you impact your personal and professional life and relationships?

  _____

  _____

Dance Reflection

Dance in the freedom of knowing that you are not your story. Put your favorite music on and let your body move to it. Write down any insights your receive and observe in your body and dance.

_____

_____

_____

_____

4

The Power of a Story

Stories can hurt, Stories can heal

What We Focus on Grows

Stories are powerful. What we plant within ourselves and our stories grows, when we feed it with our attention, conversation, thoughts, and feelings. Every time we talk, discuss, think, or feel the emotions, we are feeding it energy. As a result, we produce more of whatever we are cultivating. The stories we create and believe to be true get bigger and more real with our attention.

Have you ever noticed when you are talking about something to a friend, cohort, or family member, you relive the event? You experience the feelings, thoughts, emotions, opinions, perceptions, and beliefs. However you are seeing what happened to you, you recreate it by talking about it, thinking about it, remembering it, and reminiscing about it. You just can't seem to get it out of your head. Are you haunted by the trauma of an experience or mesmerized by the joy of it?

Every experience, whether it is positive or negative, has the possibility of developing into a story. You can distinguish your story from the word *story*. As mentioned earlier in this book, stories are everywhere in our lives. Stories are in books, movies, television, myths, fairytales, folklore, newspapers, advertisements, friendships, marriages, laws, dreams—the list goes on and on. Our story that we have integrated as part of who we are, can be seen as a thread that runs throughout our lives. Our stories grow with attention and the energy we give it, just like watering and feeding a plant. The more energy we give, the bigger it grows. The question to ask is, Is this the story I want to live my life by or would I like to change it? Remember, the truth lies behind every story.

Wherever We Go, There We Are

We take our stories with us wherever we go and wherever we are! Wherever we go—whether it is moving from the kitchen to the dining room or Hawaii to Peru—there we are. If you do not like something about where you are living and you move to a new place, you may discover that the same thing happens again. You do not like it there either.

The common denominator in this situation is you. So it is an opportunity to take a look at you. What is it that you are taking with you to your new home? A friend of mine did not like where she was living. She constantly complained about the traffic, so her family moved to a more rural area of the country. She would tell me the same *story* and complain about the new area she moved to. This time, it wasn't about the traffic, it was about the "uncultured" people. Who did she take with her? Who has the problem? She took her issue with her, because the issue was not outside of her, it was her issue, her story. What story did she take with her after moving to a new state?

We have stories about everything, everyone, and every experience. Stories begin with the way we view ourselves in terms of physical appearance, age, intelligence, success, failures, emotions, talents, experiences, relationships, and actions. The story we create is a filter that we see through in our lives. A filter is like looking through rose-colored or dark-colored glasses. We have many filters, and stories are just one of them. We ultimately choose how we see the events in our life. Every experience is viewed through our filters, boundaries, and perspective.

Stories are subjective, which means they are reflective of the individual who creates them. Stories about the same experience can differ depending upon the individual's perspective and perception. This even occurs within families. For example, the way I view my own family's health, well-being, or dysfunctionality can be seen differently through the eyes of other family members.

The common denominator for a story is you. It is you seeing your issues, emotions, feelings, thoughts, as well as your perceptions and interpretations. In other words, it is the way in which you respond to an event. There are many things that can cloud the vision of seeing the truth. Being honest with ourselves helps us to see through the barrier of our own filters. When we are honest with ourselves, we see clearly. When we know that our thoughts and feelings are just thoughts and feelings and not the truth, we can see through them. We let our hearts open and put our guard, defenses, reactions, and closed-heartedness aside. We let our heart relax and slowly be okay with everything the way it is. Knowing that nothing needs to change as we unwind and calm down. Even though we would like most things to change, we do know better.

What is a situation or circumstance that you have learned to be okay with? Knowing whatever happened is okay is the good news. A perpetrator's actions are not okay, but what happened is. In order for you to let the experience go and move past it, you need to have an open and soft heart. An open heart is important. It may not be easy to do sometimes, but know that it is possible. Let yourself heal from the past by being okay with the life event, situation, or circumstance, which simplifies the process of fighting with the thoughts, feelings, or our own stories. Being okay with your life as it is helps you to move forward and heal.

Writing and Dance Reflection

1. *Self-story*
   What is your story about yourself?

   _____

   _____

What are your thoughts and feelings about your self-concept?

_____

_____

Describe five ways your stories reflect how you see yourself.

_____

_____

_____

_____

How does your story influence and overlap with the way you see yourself, self-esteem, and self-worth?

_____

_____

How will you change as a result of changing your story?

_____

_____

We have heard stories about money, relationships, husbands, wives, partners, children, parents, grandparents, family, career, work, and the list goes on and on. Take this opportunity to self-reflect upon yourself and your stories about these aspects. Change begins with the awareness and acknowledgement of knowing and seeing the truth of your filters and boundaries. Remember that what we see is through our own "perceptual story" lens of seeing and experiencing life. The goal is to discern what is true and untrue and to know the truth behind the clouded vision of our story.

2. *What is your story about money?*

_____

_____

Do you have too much money or too little?

_____

_____

Do you work too hard or not enough?

_____

_____

How would you like to change your story about money?

_____

_____

3. *What is your story about relationships?*

_____

_____

Here are some sample questions to get you started about your present, past, and future relationships.
How do you relate to others?

_____

_____

How do you see yourself?

_____

_____

How do you think others see you in a professional relationship, friendship, or intimate relationship?

_____

_____

What kind of friend, partner, lover, husband, wife, child, parent, or grandparent are you?

_____

_____

How do you relate with those that you care and love?

_____

_____

Are you kind and patient and open and soft?

_____

_____

Do you get angry easily and hold grudges and resentments?

_____

_____

How would you like to change your story about how you relate to others and how others relate to you?

_____

_____

4. *What is your story about change?*
    Are you ready, willing, and open to it?

_____

_____

Do you fear change of the unknown?

_____

_____

What are you afraid of?

_____

_____

What is your story about resisting change?

_____

_____

How would you like to change your story about change and transformation?

_____

_____

How do you think your life will change when you become new in it?

_____

_____

5. *What is your story about career and work?*

_____

_____

What do you like and dislike about your career and/or workplace?

_____

_____

What story do you have about your coworkers and your boss?

_____

_____

How does you story impact your performance at work?

_____

_____

Describe the ways you would like to change your story about your career and work.

_____

_____

6. *What is the story about your body, health, and well-being?*

_____

_____

How would you like to exercise and improve your well-being with a conscious health program in your life?

_____

_____

Dance Reflection

Dance in the power, transformation and freedom of you. Put your favorite music on and let your body move freely. Write down any insights your receive and observe in your body and dance.

_____

_____

_____

_____

5

Excuse Me, This Is My Story

Stories make us laugh. Stories make us cry

One of the most common methods for justifying messages or communication perceived negatively is an excuse. The spoken word can be a powerful manifestation in the form of an "excuse." Excuses permeate all kinds of communication and behavior. Although the excuse applies to all human actions and behavior, we are emphasizing this role in our stories in conversation. The definition of *excuse* is an explanation or action that lessens the impact of negative implications of the individual's behavior to maintain a positive image for an individual and others.

Do You Have a Story List of Reasons and Excuses?

Stories in our lives can also serve as rationalizations, which become our reasons. Our reasons can excuse us from situations, events, experiences, and responsibilities. An example is that you do not want to go to a meeting at your workplace. You tell your supervisor you are sick or do not feel well or your child is sick when you just do not want to go to work. Even though all of these reasons are true, they are rational, reasonable stories about excusing yourself from a meeting you do not want to attend.

One of the major motives for excuse-making is to uphold our self-esteem in order to protect our self-image in the world. The goal is to protect a positive image. Excuses can also be applied to reduce the stress created by inappropriate behavior, actions or bad performance. We believe if we provide a good *excuse*, it will lessen the impact of the negative reaction and the ensuing stress that is a consequence of poor performance. We offer an excuse as a story to preserve the positive way we appear to ourselves and others. We excuse our actions, behavior, or poor performance with reasons provided in our story. The story can be completely true, but it is still "our story."

Scenario

An executive's worst fear is public speaking. This individual must address an audience of a hundred people. On the morning of this event, this person experiences a sore throat. She communicates to her supervisor that she doesn't feel very well but will give the speech regardless of how she physically feels. This story excuse is designed to lessen the criticism from herself and her supervisor, should she fail to deliver a successful speech. A healthy choice for this individual could be to acknowledge the fear of public speaking. We cannot heal what we do not acknowledge. Honesty can help us deal with the fear and turn it into a success. Feel the fear and do it regardless!

Can you think of a time when you used an excuse to feel better about yourself? When did your story get you out of work or a situation? How did your story reduce the negative consequences of the situation? How did the story decrease the stress of the circumstance? When we are writing our stories and not allowing them to write us, we gain power over them. Being aware of our stories and storytelling empowers us. We begin to realize that we are not victims when we stand in what we know. We know that our stories did not create us, we created them.

Most people love talking about themselves and sharing their opinions and stories. We all have a story to tell, and are great storytellers. The lesson here is not to make stories wrong or bad or avoid them. As humans, we naturally enjoy sharing our stories. Allowing our stories to have power over us is when the rubber hits the road. We give our power away by letting our story control who we are, our actions, and our lives. Using our stories to manipulate situations and people to get what we want or need is unhealthy. It is time to take a closer look at what we are doing. If we are using our stories to get something to make us feel better, to look good, or to avoid failure, then it is important to remember to be authentic as human beings.

Here are some suggestions to be consciously aware of our stories:

Honesty—be honest with yourself
Clarity—discern truth from untruth
Look and see with your eyes open
Pay attention
Listen to yourself
Listen to others' response and reaction to you
Listening is at the other end of telling, which is in the next chapter

Our story can be the reason for doing or not doing something. For instance, your goal is to be in better shape. You know you are overweight, out of shape, and need to workout. Knowing to do something that is good for us does not always mean we will do it. For example, you get hurt at the gym by not following the instructions on the weight machine. Every time you think about the gym, you associate it with your injury and negative experience. This becomes your story about the gym. The more you think about the gym and your experiences, the bigger it grows. You may also use this experience as your *reason* for not going to the gym, even though you know you need to exercise for better health, energy and well-being.

What was a situation or circumstance in your life that you told a story to avoid doing something? What are your reasons or excuses? Our stories allow us to place our messages, excuses, even our greatest failures, in a more favorable light. There is nothing right or wrong about making excuses or telling our stories about them. The point here is the awareness that we are doing so. Paying attention and being honest helps us to be consciously aware and grow. What do we know the truth of in our thoughts and feelings? Knowing that we are responsible for our choices, stories and excuses is powerful.

Reclaiming our Power

The knowledge that we are the creators of our reasons, excuses, and stories helps us to step back, take a look and regain our power. When we know that there is no one else to blame in a situation, we are empowered. Choosing powerfully means being mindful and 100 percent responsible for our actions. Although we may not have control over the consequences, we can choose to learn and grow from them. Being responsible and choosing powerfully means we are not being a victim of our circumstances and life occurrences. Failure to acknowledge responsibility creates a victim. Life happens. Know that we get to choose how we respond to our life experiences.

Writing and Dance Reflection

- Name the situation, issue, person, relationship, workplace, and circumstance

  _____

  _____

- What is the story you have regarding this event?

  _____

  _____

- Did you offer an excuse? If yes, explain the excuses included in your story.

  _____

  _____

- How did you avoid looking bad to yourself and others?

  _____

  _____

- What was the outcome of this event?

  _____

  _____

- How did you avoid failure by your excuses and reasons?

  _____

  _____

- If you could, would you do anything differently?

  _____

  _____

- How would you change and rewrite your story?

  _____

  _____

- How can you be honest with yourself and accept full responsibility? Draw a stick figure of you being free of your story.

  _____

  _____

  _____

  _____

Dance Reflection

Dance the story of your excuses as your story releases and moves you! Put your favorite music on and let your body move freely. Write down any insights your receive and observe in your body and dance.

  _____

  _____

  _____

  _____

6

Story as Communication

Stories can show. Stories can tell. Be ready to listen

Listening can mean giving attention with the ear or attending closely for the purpose of hearing; to perceive and/or learn through the ear

Are You a Good Listener?

Once we say something, it cannot be unsaid. Spoken words are powerful tools to use and abuse. Have you ever told someone your story and knew they weren't listening, because they were ready to tell their story? In order for a person to truly listen, they have to be present, and meet you in the moment. They must be free of agendas or any distractions.

The actual process of listening can be described in human communication as receiving, understanding, remembering, evaluating, and responding. Receiving is listening that begins with receiving the messages the speaker sends. Understanding is knowing what the speaker means, which includes thoughts, feelings, and emotional tone. Remembering the messages you receive and understanding them need to be maintained in the communication. Evaluating consists of judging the messages—in this case, the stories—in some way. Responding is providing a response to the speaker by first listening.

We can respond in the listening process by making responses while the speaker is talking or offer responses after the speaker has finished talking. When we are communicating, we are meeting the speaker by being the listener. We are in the listening of the speaker. We respond and provide information which tells the speaker that we are present to what they are speaking about. The way we listen can be influenced by gender and culture. Different cultures and genders can affect the speaker and the listener in many ways.

When the speaker and listener are from different cultures or genders, it shows in the differences between the speaker sharing the message and the listener receiving it. Culture affects the language we speak, our speech, nonverbal behavioral differences, body language, feedback, and credibility.

Research states that women use more listening cues, such as nodding in agreement and smiling, which signifies to the other person that they are paying attention and interested. Men use fewer listening cues and interrupt more. Men will often change the topic to one they know more about, one that is less relational or people oriented, or one that is more factual such as sports, statistics, and politics. Women do the same but will include details such as memories, emotions, and encouragement. Men tend to converse in a simpler way, which can appear to be clearer than a woman's conversation. Men have a more focused conversation with more intellect and less detail. Women talking to women tend to have conversations with more depth and layers than men, with each woman adding more complexity to the topic.

Active listening serves you with your understanding of what is being spoken and its meaning. Reflecting back to the speaker is an important aspect of active listening, which lets the speaker know that you acknowledge and accept the communication. For example, in listening to someone's story, you may say, "As you are telling your story, you sound angry and frustrated about the relationship breakup." The listener reflects the words they heard back to the speaker. This provides the speaker an opportunity to correct the listener and know they have been heard.

Why Is Listening So Important?

As a therapist working with adults, I learned that everyone has a deep yearning to be heard and listened to. Every week, I would see clients, and they would tell me the same story over and over again. I would ask them if they did the actions or behaviors that we discussed in the previous week. Sometimes the answer was "Yes, I followed through with your advice." Other times, the client did not take any action at all. So I would listen to their story and/or whatever new event occurred in their life. As a guidance counselor, I listened to children's stories about the death of a grandparent or their parents' divorce. Children needed their stories, feelings, and thoughts to be listened to, and they were resilient. We took action together to help them move through their difficulties and challenges.

Telling our stories engage us. Stories trigger feelings, thoughts, beliefs, and meaning when we listen to them. If talking about our stories gives us a sense of empowerment, we talk about them more. Everyone wants their voice to be heard. We want to be listened to and have others get who we are and know us through the eyes of our story. This is one of the many reasons we communicate our stories. We may want to be listened to, express ourselves through our story, or express our thoughts, feelings, and the views through our story.

Human communication is an infinite field and varies from talking to oneself to mass communication, which is talking to a number of people. Your beliefs about communication influence how you communicate with others as both sender and receiver. Your gender, culture, family history, language, personality, beliefs, opinions, values, morals, and personal expressions are just some of the factors that affect our way of communicating. Our way of communicating can be in the context of a story, and our story can be a form of communication. Communication is a key factor in language, and in language, we tell our stories. We touch others through the language of our stories. Have you ever had someone tell you their story, and now you see them in a completely different way? You understand them and get their *world* based upon their story. Your perception and view of that person changed. It is important to listen and pay attention to what you are communicating to others through your stories.

We all have a story to tell. This chapter encompasses the aspects of communication, listening, and speaking in the world of *story*. We have a story, share our story, and become a storyteller. Story and storytelling are two completely different concepts. Personal stories can become storytelling, and storytelling can become a personal story. A story in order to be a story needs to be communicated. And in order to communicate, we need a listener—whether it is ourselves or others. The purpose of this chapter is to be aware and conscious of actively participating in the world of story as a communicator, storyteller, and listener. We change roles as we tell, share, express, listen, respond, understand, and communicate our stories.

Listening to music is similar to listening to stories. Embrace the practice of being fully present to music in all its details. Like any other skill, the ability to hear the person's voice and to listen carefully grows perceptively through repetition and practice.

How Good of a Listener Are You?

Respond to each question with this scale:

1 = always 2 = frequently 3 = sometimes 4 = seldom 5 = never

- Listen by participating: So you interject comments throughout the conversation?

- I listen to what the speaker is saying and feeling: I feel what the speaker feels

- I listen without judging the speaker

- I listen to the literal meanings that a speaker communicates: I don't look too deeply into hidden meanings.

- I listen passively: I am silent and take in what the other person is saying

- I listen objectively

- I focus on the ideas logically rather than on the emotional meaning of the message.

- I listen critically, evaluating the speaker and what the speaker is saying.
- I look for the hidden meanings, the meanings that are revealed by subtle verbal or nonverbal cues.

These statements focus on the ways of listening. Review each statement and identify situations in which these statements would be appropriate or situations when they would be inappropriate.

What conclusions did you make about yourself in reference to this listening scale? Are you a good listener?

Writing and Dance Reflection
The Listener and the Storyteller

- Describe the ways in which you listen.

  _____

  _____

- Describe the ways in which you tell your story.

  _____

  _____

- How are they the same and how do they differ?

  _____

  _____

- Do you consider yourself a good listener? Explain your reasons.

  _____

  _____

- What improvements can you make with your listening skills?

  _____

  _____

- If you are not a good listener, how can you improve as a listener as mentioned in this chapter?

  _____

  _____

- Do you enjoy telling your stories more than listening? Are you telling your story to yourself while someone is telling theirs? Do you interrupt while someone is speaking to you?

  _____

  _____

  _____

  _____

- What improvements can you make to become a better listener?

  _____

  _____

- Do you enjoy listening more than telling your stories? If so, what steps can you take to express yourself more? What is your fear about expressing yourself to others?

  _____

  _____

- Can you feel the fear and learn to express yourself anyway? You can take baby steps and begin with people that you know and feel comfortable with expressing yourself.

  _____

  _____

- How can you step out of your stories and connect with what you know about it?

  _____

  _____

Dance Reflection

Listen to music. Listen and dance to music. Dance and let your body move freely to your favorite tunes. Write and describe each of these experiences. How is listening to music different from listening to someone speak? Pay attention to any message your body and dance bring forth. Write down any significant insights your receive.

_____

_____

_____

_____

7

Connecting Through Stories

Stories can connect. Stories can separate

We learned in chapter six that we communicate through our stories. In this chapter, we will discuss how we connect through our stories. Stories connect us to our humanity. As human beings, we express and interpret our world in art, paintings, songs, music, theater, movies, dance, writing, and our stories. These are some of the ways we communicate our experiences. We get to be with others and share our humanity. We gain insights regarding the human condition and its profound unique qualities.

When we watch a movie, we are connecting with the movie. We personalize the story. Cinema is the most accessible art form because of its story line. The star image is presented for its basic entertainment value. The story line depicts a relatedness that we, as human beings, can identify with in some way. The more we relate to the story, the greater the connection we feel and experience. When we identify with the characters, the actors, actresses, the setting, and the time period, the identification grows as if we are the characters and this story is happening to us. The story becomes alive in us. We are living the story of the movie. We not only feel connected to the movie, but when we share our thoughts and feelings , we invite them right into it with our story.

My fiancé and I went to see the movie *Lucy* with Scarlet Johansson. While enjoying the movie, I became the main character, Lucy, as she expanded in her awareness and consciousness. Throughout the movie, she performed above human normal actions. By the end of the movie, she was utilizing all of the capabilities and abilities of her brain. What was a movie that you became the main character or identified with its story?

Mirror, Mirror Tell Me All

Have you ever noticed that when you are with other people, who like the same things or like to do the same things that you do, you feel connected with them? More importantly, is the feeling reciprocated? Have you ever met someone and knew there was something about them that you did not like? And then you discovered the same quality in yourself? Other people can be our mirror. We see ourselves in them.

I will never forget when I graduated college, and my mother took me on a trip to Acapulco, Mexico. My mother had been ill with cancer for several years, but that year, she was strong and healthy to take a trip. We arranged our stay at the Marriott Hotel. It was a great hotel. Acapulco was a beautiful city on the Gulf of Mexico. Every day we went to the beach, I would notice a scantily clad young woman wearing a bikini. She was in her twenties, blonde, attractive, and alone! My mother, and I talked and laughed with her. In a short time, she became fond of my mother.

One day, we began talking, and she invited me to go out for the evening. As a naive and shy introvert, my mother encouraged me to go out with her and to have fun. She had met a Mexican man who had a friend, and she wanted me to go out with him. We went out to dinner, and then we got invited back to their house. I felt uncomfortable and wanted to go back to the hotel. I was not interested in being with this man. We talked and talked the evening away. We were passing time while Beverly was in the other room. I was fortunate, because his friend did not pressure me in any way to have sex with him. After several hours of waiting for my friend, I finally got back to the hotel late that night. The next day, she told us her story. Her father had passed away at a young age from heart problems, and her mother passed away from cancer. She was left without her parents in her twenties and became the sole caregiver for her younger sister. The following year, my mom passed away. I, too, was requested to be a guardian of my twelve-year-old younger brother. I had a heart-to-heart connection with this woman, who I knew for only less than a week, because of the similarities of our life story. My story reflected and mirrored hers.

This is what I call the *mirror effect*. We all mirror each other in some way. Perhaps you meet someone, and you see that they are very manipulative. They have an agenda to get something they want or need. Do you recognize the possibility of how seeing another's agenda could reflect the mirror effect?

How Do People Deflect Your Story?

How do people take you away from your story? Have you ever shared with someone and they begin to talk about themselves and in the process take you away from what you were talking about in the first place? *Deflection* means to turn away or ignore an emotional trigger to prevent full awareness of a psychological or physical area. It is an unconscious action to divert the attention of one's feelings and impulses. Some people do this by laughing instead of taking themselves seriously, endless talking or focusing their attention on the care of others. People can bring us into a closer connection with them through stories. Or, they can act in such a way that repels us and in the process, we disconnect from them.

The Body-and-Mind Connection

How does our story show up in the body-and-mind connection? Body language is a good indicator of our thoughts and feelings. We tell our story with our body language. Our bodies reflect what we are thinking and feeling through our movements, gestures, and facial expressions. The ways we are being in our body are seen in the way we move. For instance, if we are angry, these feelings will be expressed in our body language and facial expressions. We express our thoughts, feelings, intentions, emotions, and much more, through our bodies. The way we move, how we sit, how we look or not look at someone, if our legs and arms are crossed or uncrossed, the way we stand, and how we walk are just some examples of how we move in the language of our bodies.

Who we are can be seen through body language. Body language can be a flip of the hair, hands on your hips, the way you move, walk, and talk and facial expressions. Even subtle movements and gestures of your fingers, hands, and feet can express what you are thinking and feeling. How you move in your body can tell a story about you just as much as what comes out of your mouth!

Body language is unconscious. In other words, we may not realize what we are saying with our bodies. We can tell our story to others without even realizing it. When we become conscious of what our body is telling us, we can learn more about ourselves and others.

We also have body memory. Have you ever noticed that your body can remember how to do something and you don't? I witnessed this taking ballroom dance lessons with my husband. He did a foxtrot dance step and didn't even know how he did it!

Dance and body movement allows us to be in our bodies. Being physically present to our bodies allows us to be aware and shift in new ways. Through dance, we can learn new patterns and release old patterns. Through dance steps and movement, we gain body awareness as well as new ways to function and move.

Writing and Dance Reflection

Here are simple ways to gain insights and become aware of your body language and story:

1. List a life experience.

   _____

   _____

2. What is your interpretation/understanding of this experience?

   _____

   _____

3. What does it mean to you?

    _____

    _____

4. What is the story about this situation/circumstance/experience/
    event in your life?

    _____

    _____

5. What do you believe to be true about your story?

    _____

    _____

6. How do your beliefs impact your life?

    _____

    _____

7. List the ways you live by this story

    _____

    _____

8. What are you communicating about your story and yourself
    with your body language?

    _____

    _____

9. What does your body reveal about your stories?

    _____

    _____

10. What messages are being expressed in your body language?

    _____

    _____

Dance Reflection

Allow yourself to connect to your body. Be in your body and pay close attention to what you are experiencing in it. Connect to the music. What do you experience in your connecting to music? Dance as you connect to the music. Enjoy being present in the dance of connection to your body. What gifts do you receive in your connection? Write down your insights and observations.

8

Getting to the Heart of Your Stories

Stories lift our hearts. Stories break our hearts

Listening to our bodies can help us become more aware of our stories. The body knows before we do. Body intelligence is a great guide and gift. Listening and being aware of the body's needs and nourishment can impact health in a powerful way. How does your body feel? Where are your aches and pains? Are you always hungry, tired, uncomfortable? Do you have backaches, headaches, or have problems sleeping, loss of appetite? What is your body telling you? Pay attention

Whatever we take to heart, we invite into our bodies. Our hearts are an aspect of who we are, so whatever we let in, becomes part of us and lives in our hearts. When we take our stories and ourselves to heart, we internalize them into our bodies. As a dancer, I have learned that every experience in life is stored deep in the cells of the body. I know this because when I dance, different emotions arise and are released when I move. I let go of an issue or problem. This occurs naturally when I am not consciously thinking about the problem, issue, past, or circumstance. A body in motion lets body patterns shift and invites change and healing.

Through my chiropractor visits, acupuncture doctor, and cranial sacral therapist, I learned that the body is a storehouse for information. I know and experienced this when the practitioner touched body areas, I felt the point of tension and energy being released. I have experienced sadness and tears. Past experiences enter my mind as well as old wounds, pain, laughter, increased energy, freedom, clarity of thinking, ease of movement, and renewal.

I was once told by a health practitioner never to believe a doctor's diagnosis. This woman was diagnosed with lupus, bleeding in her bed, and told she had only a short time to live. She found a natural way (raw foods and whole food supplements) to heal and cure her lupus. She started a healing practice to help others heal through the same method she healed herself.

In the world of story, the health practitioner was saying not to make a story or believe what anyone tells you unless you know it is true. Now we can see how easy it is to make a story about what we are told.

What we take to heart lives deep in our bodies. Our beliefs and stories manifest themselves in our bodies. The manifestations can come in a variety of ways like diseases. Dis-ease has many forms. What we believe to be true lives in our hearts and bodies. The awareness of story is a powerful invitation for healing and growth.

My brother is another example. He was diagnosed with Hodgkin's disease. The disease went into remission for over twenty years after radiation and chemotherapy treatments. He began to have problems eating and swallowing. When he visited his lung doctor, he was told that the radiation had damaged his throat and lungs, which resulted in scar tissue growth. He drank water with every meal to help him swallow his food. His doctor also told him that there was nothing that could be done. If his throat was operated on, it would eventually grow more scar tissue. If he had a lung transplant, he would only live two years. My brother took to heart what the doctor told him. He responded by believing that nothing was possible to reverse the damages to his throat and lungs. His emotional response was denial and depression regarding his illness. He continued to live his life despite his physical challenges and difficulties. He also knew of a woman who had had the same disease and was doing well in remission. Eventually, he developed pulmonary fibrosis, chronic bronchitis, and lung infections. One time, he was home alone and had an almost fatal choking episode. He called 911 and was rushed to the emergency room. A few months later, it happened again. Only this time, the hospital staff suspected heart problems. He was tested for an enzyme in his blood prior to having a heart attack. The next day, he had a stint put in his heart. He came home and was not getting better. A few weeks later, he ended up back in the emergency room, was put on life support, and within several weeks, he passed away.

I shared this story to give you an example of how powerful believing our stories can be. Yes, his death can be looked at as it was meant to be his time or his fate. And yes, the doctor's prognosis about his condition maybe true. The point I am making is about self-resignation and not doing anything about a condition. It is sad but true that my brother did not take responsibility for his own health and well-being. He took to heart what his doctor told him. He believed his prognosis of not being able to heal his condition. I gave him alternative health recommendations and spent money on supplements, but he refused to take them. I found them on his shelf years later. He just gave up! What we believe to be true is powerful. Our beliefs impact our bodies, hearts, minds, and well-being.

What We Believe to Be True Becomes Our Reality

This is another example. I once participated in an experience, where people became aware of physical discomfort in their bodies. They were quiet for ten to fifteen minutes, breathing and relaxing. A leader guided them to look at their physical aches and uneasiness, and he challenged them to experience the pain in a new way. The leader asked, "How many hands felt a difference after this exercise?" Seventy percent of the people raised their hands. What does this exercise say about believing our stories and the effect they have on our bodies and minds?

Writing and Dance Reflection

1. What story have you taken to heart?

   _____

   _____

2. Did this story break your heart? List the ways you took this story to heart.

_____

_____

3. How has this affected you physically?

_____

_____

4. How has what you have taken to heart affected you emotionally and mentally? What is your body language telling you about what is at the heart of your story?

_____

_____

5. Do you feel any aches and pains, soreness?

_____

_____

6. How does your body respond when you are sharing, thinking or emotionally responding to your story?

_____

_____

Here are some more questions to ask yourself:

• What story lifts your heart?

_____

_____

• How is your body responding when you think, feel or talk about your story?

_____

_____

- Where is the tension in your body?

  _____
  _____

- Do you feel heaviness or lightness in your body?

  _____
  _____

- Describe ways to express your happy heart.

  _____
  _____

- How would you like to change or rewrite your story?

  _____
  _____

Dance Reflection

Let dance take you out of your mind and into your body. As you move your body, be in your heart. Let your heart move your body. Dance and let go of your story. Move with the passion of the tango, the romance of the rumba or the fun of the swing.

_____
_____
_____
_____

9

Are You Stuck in Your Story?

Stories echo our past. Stories from the past can create our future.

Are you aware that you are even stuck in your story with yourself and your life? When we are honest with ourselves we know. When we are dishonest with ourselves, we focus on our wants and needs. Being truthful and honest with ourselves is the way out of being stuck in our story. Discover ways to become unstuck in your story by answering the following questions: Is your world full of confusion? Are you having challenges finding the truth in a situation or being honest with yourself? Do you find it difficult to change or to do things differently? Do the same situations happen over and over again? Do you think the same thoughts and feel the same feelings in referencing a particular person, issue, problem, circumstance, and/or situation? Do you want to forget the past or a situation?

If you have answered yes to several of these questions, you could be trapped. Being stuck means a variety of things. You can be stuck, obsessed, infatuated, enthusiastic, or be wild about someone or something. You have heard of the idioms, such as being stuck-up, stuck in traffic, and stuck on someone and something. Being stuck in your story means that you stay in the same place. You are not moving forward. You are playing the same song over and over again. Have you ever thought about what it would be like to be in quicksand? You may be sinking down into the earth, unaware that you are even going in that direction. Wanting to keep everything under our control keeps us stuck. The first step is the knowledge of being stuck. My term for that is "being stuck in the muck." Being stuck can feel sticky like tar or bubble gum. Every time we try to move or do something new and different, we can't budge or we are too afraid. When we decide to move, our story moves with us. We are unable to leave it behind and move forward. Everything that is keeping us stuck is sticking to us like glue.

Being honest releases us from the entrapment and confines of being stuck. Honesty helps us to find the truth in what we know. When you are honest about this situation what do you know? Are you being led by the way you want or need the story to be a certain way? I realized that wherever I went, there I was. It did not matter if I was in the living room or the kitchen; wherever I went, I took me! And not only did I take me, I also took my story! When I realized that I had a story that I was stuck in, I knew to be okay with it.

One story that I have been stuck in most of my life is the story of making and receiving money. I have traced this experience back to growing up as a child. I was conditioned into thinking that I was a girl, and that was different than being a boy. I had two brothers and a baby brother at the time. I compared myself to what they were able to do and I was not able to do—all because I was girl. Why do I have to do the dishes? "You are the girl," my mother would tell me. Why do I have to come home early? "You are the girl," I was told. When I asked what career path I should follow, I was told, "You are a girl. You will grow up, get married, and have children." Yes, that was in the 1960s to 1970s, but those words are still running deep in my subconscious mind.

Realize that you have the ability to move past your story and step into something new. Our stories run deep within us, sometimes, we are unable to access them. I am not suggesting that you begin psychoanalysis to discover your hidden stories. Begin to be more aware of your thoughts, feelings, and your way of being.

My money story pertains to all of my "free" classes and presentations. I share my gifts and knowledge and enjoy getting paid for my time and expertise. My passion is the fire of inspiration, love, knowing the truth and giving to others.

I know that I need to earn money for survival on this planet. I manifest abundance doing what I love dancing, writing, creativity, healing with art, workshops and inspirational presentations. I am creating a new relationship with success. But I still get butterflies in my stomach talking about it. The body does not lie, and the body always knows first. So if and when you feel something within your body, pay attention to it.

Stepping past my story included attending a workshop and following a plan on the ways to write a nonfiction book in four weeks. My intention focus and deliberate actions resonated with the completion of writing this book. So in the process, I am rewriting my story of success. My recreated story is to become a successful author on the best seller list, an inspirational speaker, and make a contribution to society.

We can use our stories to get what we want and manipulate situations and others. Our stories can be so a part of who we are and what we identify with that we cannot separate the two. In this process, we find ourselves living and acting from our stories. Are we able to go back to the beginning of our story to where it began or started? How did we get to where we are now? Or we can be honest with ourselves and follow our deepest knowing about our story, ourselves and our life.

As I mentioned earlier in this book, one of my earliest stories began after my father passed away. Watching my father die right in front of me was terrifying and traumatic as a child. I could feel the impact in my body. As an adult, I feared that being with a man, I would watch him die—the same that happened when I was a child. For ten years, I avoided being in a relationship. I was too afraid because of past choices and experiences. By being honest with myself, I began to transform my beliefs about relationships and open my heart. In order to open my heart, I had to let my walls down and let go of my story.

Stepping Out of My Story

A huge step out of my story happened a few weeks ago at the artist therapy session. I have been going to see an art therapist for several months. I love the creative arts. I enjoy creating, dancing, painting, writing, cooking, and having new ideas and innovations. The last session was on the anniversary of my father's death. She asked me to follow the "trauma map."

I drew pictures not just for the sake of art, but also because I was moved and inspired to draw pictures based upon the words on each page. Each picture was more about what came to me and from my experience, rather than the artwork itself. As each word was stated, I drew the picture that came to me and used the materials I gravitated toward. I used crayons and pastels to draw the following words for this experience: startle, thwarted intention, the freeze, altered state, body sensation, automatic obedience, and self-repair. After drawing each picture, I hung them on the bulletin board. I examined and reviewed the artwork in each picture, which represented my experience. Each picture told a story of my interpretation of what had happened to me as a child. The artwork offered and provided deep insights on another level that bypassed the conscious mind. "Art," she told me, "comes from the unconscious or even the subconscious mind's dreams. Art never tells us what we already know. Art always tells us something new and what we need to know."

I learned so much about myself, my parents, and this experience through the artwork and the traumatic words applied in progressive stages. In the beginning of this art experience, I could feel that a lingering pain in my heart and body that was still there. After completion of this art exercise, I felt a release, and the pain had disappeared through this process. Art was the medium that I used to move past my story and free myself of the story about my father's death.

Be Part of the Solution and Not Part of the Problem

- *Awareness*

  I became aware of the story I created around my father's death. Through this awareness, I had a deeper willingness to move past it. Becoming aware of your story is powerful to know what we are living in, seeing through, and creating our future from.

- *Willingness*

  I had a willingness to allow any pain to come up, to feel and heal, and move past my story. How? For the simple reason of paying attention, knowing, looking, seeing, listening, and responding. Allow your heart to be filled with willingness and openness. Even when you do not understand, keep your heart open.

- *Clearing*

  Clearing the space of your story is being unfiltered in what you know is true in and about your story. Release and let go of your thoughts, feelings, emotions, actions, and the ways you are responding to your story. You can choose to clean the space that holds your story. If you buy new furniture, you need to remove the old furniture first before you can replace it.

- *Intention*

  I knew in my heart that it was time to move forward and let go of the past. Intention is a powerful tool that offers a focus and a way of being within ourselves. You know that you need to do something, and you follow straight to it. You act upon your knowledge.

- *Knowing*

  We know that no matter how painful it is, we can move past it. In the process, we create a new opportunity for ourselves. We can live from a new place. You can begin by listening to what you know the truth of in your heart. What is the knowing in your heart that you need to let go of and move forward? State the intention and the desire.

Do You Find Yourself Controlling with the Drama of Your Story?

Stories come in many forms. Here is an example of how we use our stories. Control is a part of being human. We all want things to go our way, we want to control them. Letting go and letting things take on their own course or letting people be who they are as they are is difficult and challenging. We want to change other people, things, situations, circumstances, ourselves, and our life. One of the ways we do this is through our stories.

A good example is a mother who consistently has problems with her child. The child has a behavior problem with emotional issues from a divorce. The mother has a full-time job. She constantly and consistently uses her son's disabilities to excuse herself from her workplace. This shows up in her being late every day.

Or, you do not want to attend a meeting on Monday. You wake up and do not feel very well. You do not feel well, but you feel good enough to go to work. You tell your boss that you are sick and not able to come to work. The result is you get what you want. You get out of going to the meeting and not going to work that day.

- *Blame Story*

  The blame game is a story that does not exist in truth. We made that one up. It is a story we created and believed to make us feel better. Whenever someone places blame on others, in truth, it is to escape responsibility. Blame occurs in personal and professional areas of our life, between couples, parents, and children, within the workplace, divorce, politics, and religion. Blame happens everywhere we place it.

- *Shame Story*

  People are shamed for their feelings, thoughts, and behavior as well as for their culture, race, religion, morality, gender, etc. We can feel shame about our feelings, thoughts, and actions. Shame is defined as a painful feeling of humiliation or distress caused by the consciousness of wrong behavior. Shame happens when we think we did something wrong, or think there is something wrong with us. When we think and feel there is something wrong with us, we live from a place of shame revealed in our stories and life.

- *Stress Story*

  Stress is our response to a life event causing pain and upset or joy. We can or cannot do certain things in our lives because of the everyday stress and anxiety that challenges us. Just the mere thought about what we need to do may cause a stressful reaction and stop us in our tracks. We can create stories about our reaction to a stimulus that disturbs our physical and mental equilibrium and triggers a flight-or-fight response. We may not be able to control the stressors in our life, but we can change and control our responses, reactions and our stories.

  What is a stressor in your life? What is your story about it? How does it stop you from doing what you really want to do? What can I do to deal with the stressor/s in my life in a healthy way? How can I rewrite my stress story for the joy or sadness in my life and enhance my health and well-being?

- *Family Story*

  Who does not have a story, either positive or negative, to tell about their family relationships? What is a family story that you talk about? Are there really two sides to a story? Yes, the two sides of a story involve the two perspectives. Two perspectives mean two points of view. The two perspectives are the two ways of seeing the same event.

Perspective includes the way we see ourselves, others, and the world. Perspective also takes our belief system into account. Our belief system is created from our past experiences, culture, values, and current situation. Can you see how beliefs, perspectives, interpretations and the meaning of an experience/event can write your story?

Perception is the interpretation from the five senses, touch, smell, sight, hearing, and taste. Perception is the process of an awareness or understanding of sensory information. When we put ourselves in another's perspective, it changes the perception of life. In other words, when we put ourselves in someone else's shoes, we see things differently, and our reality shifts. Do our perspectives come from our perceptions or do our perspectives come from our perceptions? What do you think?

Event–perception–perspective–interpretation–meaning–story–belief

- *Relationship Story*

Is the person in the beginning of a relationship the same at the end? Is the person we marry the same person we divorce? Changes occur naturally as the relationship progresses. You can ask yourself: Have I grown in a healthy way and learned from the relationship? Or, am I living in my story about it?

For example, when a husband and wife blame each other for their divorce, neither are being responsible. How do blaming stories serve us? We do not have to be responsible or make any changes if it is someone else's fault! When we are honest, we know that we are responsible for our choices and actions. Trust your inner guidance and knowing.

A story I had for many years was regarding the loss of my parents at an early age. Not only did I share the event but I also shared my story about it. I lost my childhood. I did not have my parents at my graduation, wedding, and major events in my life. What I was getting from others was sympathy, understanding, compassion, and empathy. Being aware of my actions and the acceptance of these events, healed my pain. Now, when I share my life and events, I have no expectations.

Pay attention and become aware of the stories you share most often. Listen to how you share and tell your story. Know the difference of what we can change and what we cannot change. You are the only common denominator. With every situation, there you are.

Remember, stories are okay. It is when we believe our stories and see how they prevent us from our good and evolution, then it is time for change. Stories cloud our vision about ourselves and our world. The truth is, the only one we can change is ourselves. When the perception of ourselves changes, our perspective with everything changes. We cannot change our boss, spouse, lover, friends, family members, and employees. Clearing our cloudy vision and the pathway of our heartfelt stories, we experience a lightness of the heart. When we allow ourselves to be who we truly are, we let our light shine!

- *Purposeful Stories*

  For what purpose do you use your stories?
  How do they serve you and your life?
  What do you gain by having this story?
  What is your controlling drama?
  How do you gain control with your controlling drama?
  Do you get people's full attention?
  Are your underlying goals/intentions the real reasons for creating and controlling this story?
  Do you get more attention, receive a pity party, excuses, avoid responsibility, feel sorry for yourself, or avoid being accountable?

Moving Past Your Story

Are you ready to be aware of your stories and dramas and be conscious of them? Allowing ourselves to really take a look at them means doing so with an open and honest heart. It is very easy to lie to ourselves. Remember that as humans, we naturally serve ourselves. We are egocentric and self-centered. This is an opportunity to move past the natural tendency to be self-centered. This means not putting ourselves and our wants and needs first. This is an opening to grow, evolve, and move forward in who we really are and create a life based on something real and not what we made up. When we feel uncomfortable and out of our comfort zone, we know we are growing.

Growing involves pain. The teenage hormones are raging and wanting so badly to act like an adult. The teenager is stifled and not of age to drive or drink. The teenager is unable to do whatever he or she wants. They become frustrated, angry and upset because life is happening and they have no control over it. The teenage "inner self" is subjected to the gauntlet of transitioning into becoming an adult.

Even if our teenage years were miserable, we can powerfully choose to move past those painful years and move forward. As horrific as our experiences are in life, we get to choose. In making a new choice, we shift and become someone new. We become different as a result of our choosing to be different in a particular story, issue, situation, etc. For example, if we revisit our teenage years with a full or conscious awareness, we may be able to see things differently. Based upon what we know now about being an adolescent and teenager and having moved past that stage in our lives, we are able to rewrite this story and heal ourselves in the process. When we reinterpret our stories based upon what we know is true about them, we can set ourselves free and move past them.

We all have stories to tell and share with each other. We tell our stories and our stories tell us. But we get to choose what will happen in the future. We cannot change our past, family, history, choices or experiences. I have gone back into the past and uncovered where the stories and patterns began, and I have shifted by consciously, choosing to be honest, following what I know and being new.

Writing and Dance Reflection

What choice can I make now regarding a situation or my story about it?

_____

_____

Know that I get to choose to be in integrity.
How can I get out of being stuck in the muck of my story?

_____

_____

I powerfully choose to let go, release and move forward in my life.
Am I ready and willing to make the difference for myself?

_____

_____

Am I committed to doing whatever it takes to move forward even if it is painful?

_____

_____

What do I need to do to fulfill my promise to myself?

_____

_____

How can I move forward and shift my way of being?

_____

_____

Dance Reflection

Dance in and through your stuck stories. You can do a percussive movement by stomping your feet on the floor. When you are finished, you can glide gracefully across the floor in the freedom of release and renewal. Write and reflect about your experiences.

_____
_____
_____
_____

10

The Courage to Release Your Story

Stories make us strong. Stories make us weak.

As we learned in chapter nine, we can get stuck in our story. This means that even if it serves us in some way, it can hurt us in other ways. Life happens. Our experiences, thoughts, and feelings can interfere with our interpretation of the real event. Perceptions and perspectives also play a big part in seeing a life event. We create a life around our story based upon our beliefs, thoughts, feelings, interpretations, and the meaning we give it. Another interesting fact is that our beliefs about situations and people also attract others to support the same belief. Have you ever wondered why people, situations, and/or relationships with similar beliefs have been showing up in your life? Or, we end a relationship, repeat the patterns and the same person appears with a different face. Have you left a workplace because of a particular situation and/or circumstance and found a new job? After the honeymoon period ended at the new job, did the same situation/circumstance come up again for you? Remember, wherever you go, there you are!

Stories are very powerful, because once we realize that we created a story, we can change it. We can choose to let go of the story or rewrite it completely. We can empower ourselves by the truth of what we know about an event or situation. We change by focusing on what is true rather than what we believed to be true. We transform as we focus, time, and energy on what is real, and we grow into being healthy human beings

In writing this book, I transform in my creative expression. I grow and change in my sharing my stories and life experiences. Being creative has always made my heart sing and my feet dance! I love dancing and writing since childhood. I remember dancing in recitals and performances and writing my mother letters. I turned my story inside out from *I couldn't* to *I can*. I created the possibility to live my passion, and write, dance, paint, and create. And now I am doing what I love to do and following my passion. Have the courage to take a real look at the distinction of what is really true and what is believed to be true.

According to Science Daily, eyewitnesses are not as reliable as one might believe. Contrary to popular belief, a person's memory of an event is not improved by retelling the story. Instead, the risk of an incorrect account increases the more the story is retold and discussed.

What Is Courage?

Courage gives a person the ability and willingness to confront fear, pain, danger, uncertainty, or intimidation. Physical courage can be facing physical pain and hardship. Moral courage is the ability to know the difference between right and wrong and to act rightly in the face of fear, opposition, shame, guilt, scandal, or discouragement. Courage enables you to follow your dreams, insights, and goals. You have the courage to be authentic and tell the truth. Courage is the bravery that affects our lives in many ways. Courage is our guide to help us move through difficulty, change, and challenges amidst our fears. We may be afraid to speak our thoughts, express our feelings, or act in certain ways.

Self-expression comes in many forms beyond speaking, such as body language, gestures, eye movements, and contact. Courage helps us to be able to express ourselves in a variety of ways. The way we are being is also a form of self-expression. As human beings, we know we enjoy communicating who we are and our state of being in the form of stories. We love to tell our stories, listen to others' stories, write stories, watch stories, and express ourselves through stories.

Metaphors can be in the form of a story. We have the courage to share ourselves with others. Some people understand what we are communicating when we tell our stories. Stories serve a wonderful purpose. Sharing our stories can bring up our fears, uncomfortable feelings and thoughts, and relive painful events of the past. The courage to communicate and express ourselves through our stories can be a wonderful experience for us.

Self-expression, communicating feelings, and asking for what I want has always been difficult for me. The realization of the anxiety and fear in my self-expression has helped me to move forward. When I have the opportunity to express myself, I begin with the pronoun I. "I feel sad about what happened. I would like for us to go to the beach today." Using the pronoun *I* is responsible communication. I have learned to be okay with self-expression. Whatever our fears are, we can move past them. Courage can help guide us.

Know the Difference between Being and Having

We live in the world of *having*. Having is the world filled with the consumption of materials, getting and buying things. "What is in it for me? Why should I do this? What will I get from it?" Our interest lies in fulfilling our wants and needs. There will always more to get and have. We are beings, not the haves or have nots (like the television show).

We can choose to be in what is right now. How can we move from having, wanting, and getting to being in the moment? We can drop and move into our hearts and just be. Get quiet inside and outside ourselves and listen. Being with nature is a great teacher. Being okay with everything exactly the way it is, is the "knowing" that nothing needs to change. As human beings, we get to be like a tree. We experience this firsthand when we relax, quiet our body and minds, and be with what is right now. This may take practice, and relaxing into your heart will help you.

Unwinding the tightly-wound-up physical, emotional, and mental focus can take some time, as well as deep breathing, being in nature, being in the moment, relaxing the body and mind in your favorite way. This can mean taking a bath, walking, biking, hiking, listening to music, dancing, working out at the gym, being creative, and enjoying being at home in whatever you are doing. This is the beginning of the subtle shift of being. Part of the unwinding begins with the unraveling of our story. We can choose to discern the unbiased, objective facts instead of listening to our thoughts, feelings, and judgments, and reactions to it. It takes courage to be profoundly honest with ourselves. Being truthful about knowing that our story is not who we are. And deep within us, we know that we are not our story and we can let it go. We get to be in our hearts, knowing and being beneath the surface.

Being honest and objective with the facts and circumstances in my life was painful. Knowing and seeing the truth in what I had done to myself was not a pretty picture, especially the way I manipulated others. The truth and healing is painful at any cost. There is a price for growth and evolution. In order for us to move forward, we have to leave something behind, and be new, which can be uncomfortable and painful. Let courage be the guide to heal old hurts and deep wounds.

Have the courage to be brave as you become honest with yourself. Give yourself permission to peel yourself away from your story. Know that you do not need it anymore for any reason. Even if it is a juicy one and one that you get a lot from it, let it go.

The story that you created with true facts maybe be hurting more than helping you. Your story can be hurting you even if you-get something from it such as excuses, or avoidance of responsibilities. You will be freer and healthier without it! Enjoy the courage of self-expression, the desire that lies deep within the heart of all human beings. Know that fear is not real. Our fears do not come of anything but the truth that we know of. As soon as we are profoundly honest and know what is true, our fears disappear, and goodness and love appears.

Writing and Dance Reflection

Be honest and truthful with yourself about the situation and circumstance. If the situation and your story are the same, then look at the ways that your story is holding you back from moving forward in that area in your life. What do you know about the situation, event, and circumstance? Listen to your heart and know that everything is okay exactly the way it is.

Take deep breaths and breathe into releasing the hold your story has on your body and mind. Clearing the space is like erasing a whiteboard and having a blank slate to begin anew. The only power our story has over you is one you give it. Whatever we feed and give energy to grows. Be powerful in letting go and/or rewriting your story. Know that within every life situation is a golden nugget, a loving lesson of truth within it. Know that goodness is present in every moment. Sometimes during the most painful events, we learn the greatest lessons. Pain does not feel very good, but know that it is only pain and goodness remains.

Ways to become aware of your story:

1. Describe a life experience that needs courage.

   _____

   _____

2. What is your interpretation/understanding of this experience?

   _____

   _____

3. What did you make it mean? What does it mean to you?

   _____

   _____

4. What is the story about this situation/circumstance/experience/ event in your life?

   _____

   _____

5. How will you become a stronger person dealing with this event and story?

_____

_____

6. Do you believe your story?

_____

_____

7. How does this story affect your life?

_____

_____

8. Have the courage to list the ways to let go of this story. How will changing this story change your life?

_____

_____

Ways to step out of your story:

1. Know that your story is self-created and made-up

_____

_____

2. Know that it is okay that the event happened.

_____

_____

3. Be courageous. Open your eyes to a new way of seeing the event as just an event.

_____

_____

4. Know that there is a difference between the event and the story about the event.

_____

_____

5. Be honest. Although you have beliefs about your story, know the truth, you created it.

_____

_____

6. Write down the facts about the event.

_____

_____

7. Discern the difference between what is true about what happened and the meaning you gave it.

_____

_____

8. Take a close look at how you live your life, believing the story and *not* the event.

_____

_____

9. Love and do not punish or be negative to yourself for creating a story.

_____

_____

10. Know that you can live seeing life through a new lens and new eyes

_____

_____

Dance Reflection

Dance your intentions!
Dance your goals!
What is your intention in reading this book, dancing, and journal writing?

_____

_____

Write down 4 goals.

_____

_____

_____

_____

Write your accomplishments.

_____

_____

11

Do Your Stories Empower You?

Stories can heal, stories can hurt.

When do stories hurt, and when do stories help?

> *"A story is not like a road to follow…it's more like a house. You go inside and stay there for a while, wandering back and forth and settling where you like and discovering how the room and corridors relate to each other, how the world outside is altered by being viewed from these windows. And you, the visitor, the reader, are altered as well by being in this enclosed space, whether it is ample and easy or full of crooked turns, or sparsely or opulently furnished. You can go back again and again, and the house, the story, always contains more than you saw the last time. It also has a sturdy sense of itself of being built out of its own necessity, not just to shelter or beguile you."* Alice Munro

Helpful Stories

As humans, we live in the world of story. From the beginning of human history, we have been told stories of cavemen and cavewomen and Adam and Eve. These stories have been passed down and told to us in the early cave paintings, ancient artworks, and artifacts from our human ancestors. A defining characteristic of being human is to leave s sign or mark that we were there at this point in time. This mark can be defined as a painting, wood or stone carving, architectural structure, and pictures words such as hieroglyphics or cuneiform writing that tell stories. We have the stories of mythology, a hero's journey, and the archetypes of ancient and modern history. We have stories told to us by our mothers and fathers, grandmothers and grandfathers, aunts, uncles, siblings, family members, and educators. Movies, songs, poetry, and books all have stories in them.

Stories are beneficial and serve us in many ways. As human beings, we identify with stories and learn from them. We learn what to do and not to do. Stories affect us in a variety of ways; they demonstrate who we are and who we are not. Stories inspire us and serve many purposes. We have the story of marriage and romance. We have the stories of divorce and single life. Stories are everywhere from the beginning of the human race, since human beings created stories through pictures, drawings, and writings.

We know that a story can be defined as: a narrative, either true or fictitious, in prose or verse, designed to interest, amuse, or instruct the listener, or reader; a tale. A story is a fictitious, tales, shorter and less elaborate than a novel, such as a branch of literature, the plot or succession of incidents of a novel, poem, and drama. A story may not be what we think it is.

A story can be a true story. A story can be fantasy or made-up. A story can be influential. A story can be persuasive, but a story does not tell us what to do, how to feel, or what to think. A story invites us to imagine, feel, believe, and remember experiences, memories, and things that might otherwise merge into a cloud of messages that we forgot. In business, research suggests that the most engaging managers, who stand above from their peers, have the ability to share context and understand their employees, giving them emotional coloring that makes the journey of the future real, believable, and imaginable.

The beauty of stories and storytelling is that everyone knows a good story. Is the best story the one we tell our ourselves? We have seen and heard our own stories and others' stories many times. Whether we realize it or not, we can understand a story much easier than a list of facts. The world of story is the way humans communicate naturally. Our life is framed in stories. Wherever we go and whatever we do, stories are born and come alive. They help us to know, learn, grow, and understand ourselves and our world. Is that why we create them?

When we share a life event, we create a story by weaving our insights, feelings, thoughts, beliefs and opinions into it. We add our own emotional colors and flavors. Our stories become more colorful and exciting, and we call them our own. We are the main character in the story, and we know our place in it. We buy into our stories. We believe our stories. They serve us. They serve a purpose—our purpose.

Old Shoe Syndrome

The shoes on our feet represent a metaphor for our stories. Some people wear their shoes until they are so worn out, they cannot wear them anymore. They may comfortable, falling apart and old but we wear them anyway. We use and hold on to our stories in the same way. This is what I call the "Old Shoe Syndrome." We become used to the shoe comfort, and as stinky as it may be, it holds our feet in a "worn-out" way. This old shoe, like our stories, becomes part of who we are. The old shoe becomes a normal way of being. We may say to ourselves, "This is who I am and the way I act". We hide behind our stories like an old worn-out shoe and protect ourselves with them. We utilize our stories in many ways. It is like wearing a raincoat to keep us dry instead of getting drenched in the downpour of our stories.

Difficulties arise when we see what we are doing and attempt to change our patterns. We are so comfortable in a "worn-out way" that being different creates discomfort and unfamiliarity. This may cause us to return to our old ways, habits, and patterns. This is how our stories can hurt us with ourselves, others, and in our life. Can we change? With an awareness of the desire to change, a conscious effort, and a commitment to do the work, the answer is yes!

When Stories Hurt Us?

Every day, we share our stories, and, have the choice to stay in our stories or release them. You can let go of your story and create a new possibility. You can be new and different in your story. How can you rewrite your stories to match a new way of being? It is like learning a new dance and listening to an old song. Does dancing to the rhythms of an old song help you to move forward? Stories take up space in the "dance of life." When we become aware of our story, we can let it go. Letting go is a process that begins with our realization that we are in a story. Every time we talk and tell our story, it grows. When we are being different in our stories, we change.

Creating from the same space, creates more of the same. Being fresh and new means letting go of an old way of being. For example, when we are in our "I do not like my job" story or" relationship" story, we are being our familiar self. We talk about our opinions, perceptions and preferences. Remember what we give energy to grows.

When we let go of our stories, a space opens and we are able to create something new. We learn to be responsible for the lesson and occurrence in our lives. Each moment offers a golden opportunity of goodness that moves us forward. We know there is goodness that lies deep within all circumstances. Some experiences are excruciatingly painful; however, no matter how painful or joyous, there is a lesson to be learned in that transformational moment.

Our stories hurt us the most when we believe them. When we believe our stories, we make them real. The event was real, and yes, the event happened to you. Belief means "being sure that someone or something exists or that something is true, a feeling that something is good, right or valuable, a feeling of trust in the worth or ability of someone," according to the *Miriam-Webster Dictionary*. How does this definition of belief translate and relate to your story? This definition of belief gives your story more power than it deserves. Belief makes your story believable, real, good, right, valuable, and worthy. Is your story believable, real, good, right, valuable, and worthy of all the time and energy you spend on it? Does your story match this definition in all aspects? If not, what are the elements of this definition that do not apply to your story? In other words, is your story worthy of all that you make it out to be? Does it serve you or make you feel better? Does it help you to become a better person?

Here is an opportunity for you to look at whether or not your stories are helping or hurting you. If it takes away from who you really are, know that you are not your story. The facts in your story may have happened to you, but they are not you. How does your story hurt or enhance your self-worth, esteem, and image? Take a moment to reflect on a story that impacts the way you see yourself.

When we get really honest with ourselves, we know that we are the one stopping our own flow of goodness. We do this in the ingenious way of self-sabotage. We make believe that we do not know and do not see the truth. In the game of hide-and-seek, we hide from ourselves. We know what we are doing. Even if it means that what we are doing is preventing our own good, we do it anyway. Now is the time to stop playing hide-and-seek and remember that you can choose powerfully and get out of your own way!

Getting Down to the Bare Bones

Getting down to the bare bones means diving into the nitty gritty of ourselves, getting naked and being honest. This is a good time to take a look at ourselves, our life, relationships, and the past. Honesty gives us the clarity to see. Clarity gives us the vision to discern what we know the truth of. Digging deep and getting naked with ourselves can be a scary process, but it is well worth the pain. Pain is like a can opener that takes us deeper into who we really are. We grow and change. Our uniqueness and differences are told in our stories. What are you telling yourself right now as you are reading this paragraph? Quickly, write it down. Do not delay! Describe the ways you procrastinate and put off doing things until tomorrow.

Procrastination is on the top of my list for random acts of self-sabotage. "I will do it later, tomorrow, next week, month, year!" These are all the lies I tell myself to prevent my own success from happening. I do it to myself over and over again, year after year! I will write books next year, in the future, sometime! This goal was always ahead or in front of me, never right now in the present.

How Did I Stop and Gain Control over this Pattern in My Life?

When I got really honest with myself, I realized that I was a procrastinator. And the truth was I was responsible for the results and the effects it had in my life. With the awareness of what procrastination was doing to me, I stopped. I knew I had to embrace what I was doing and have the courage to change it. You can't change what you do not recognize and acknowledge. I hired a personal coach to help me identify what I needed to change in my life. She encouraged me to do an abandonment and recovery program for twelve weeks. I almost said no, because I knew I had done so much psychology and self-healing programs. I felt as though I didn't need any help in this area until I began doing it. I realized that my dreams were buried in a past of pain, hurt, loss, and death. After participating in this program, my dreams started to come alive again. I had many aha moments in the realization that by being abandoned, I had abandoned myself. I can no longer blame anyone for my past, present, future or my stories. I am an empowered, woman not a little girl with a painful past.

In uncovering the lost parts of myself, I recovered and gained a sense of power and responsibility. I was not dancing to my inner rhythm and had lost touch with a precious part of myself. I began to dance from the inside out as my innermost being moved through my self and person. I have participated in a variety of programs and educational seminars. These transformational programs helped me realize my inner truth, goals, dreams, and commitments. I set myself free to focus on my gifts and talents as an entrepreneur, author, dance instructor, facilitator and inspirational speaker.

The transformational part of my journey came several years ago. I received several messages to give up my life as I knew it. At the time, this made no sense. I listened and did it anyway. I gave up my traditional life, which included my husband, house, car, dog, and professional job. I knew what was next when I moved forward. After letting go of my traditional life, the message was to visit Maui, Hawaii. After attending two seminars on Maui, I knew my next step was to move there. During this phase of my life, I cried and cried. Letting go was a painful process. I felt as if I was still moving with blinders on and in the dark. It was like being on a game board and not into playing the game. I continued to follow my inner knowledge and guidance and moved to Maui with $1,000, seven suitcases, no job, and no place to live. All of my fears were in my face. I remember standing in the airport saying, "Okay, universe, I know I am supposed to be here. Please show me what is next." I called a friend that I met at the rebirthing and long life seminar several months before. She invited me to stay at her apartment. When I arrived at her place, she was packing boxes and moving to Honolulu. She quit her job as a substance abuse therapist and gave me the contact information to interview for this position, And the name of a woman looking for a roommate. I had the qualifications with my educational credentials and experience, and was offered the position with a new roommate. Her place was only a few blocks away from the location of my friend's apartment. This was one of my greatest lessons in trusting and following my inner guidance. I also learned the importance of stepping into what I knew and moving forward, even if I did not understand the reasons all of this was happening to me.

Dancing helped me to integrate all the changes and new ways of being into my life. I loved learning Hula and chanting from real Hawaiians who lived up on Haleakala, the dormant volcano. Moving forward in what I knew helped me to realize that I was stuck in my story. I was responsible for hurting and holding myself back. My life was crumbling before my eyes. Honesty held my hand in this realization that I was the one who put myself in this story, and I was the one who could get myself out. I realized that I was fully responsible for both the beginning and the end of my life story. If I did not listen and follow my heart, I would not have had the opportunity to meet, evolve, and learn from a master teacher of truth for many years. I created a new possibility of being committed to the power of knowing. I know when it is time for me to move forward. I know that I am responsible to set goals. And, there is no one else who can fulfill them. No, my parents are not coming back to save or rescue me. I finally realized that I do not need any help. I am a big girl now and a responsible adult capable of taking care of herself.

Divorce Story

Your parents got a divorce when you were twelve years old. As an adult, you remember the pain of the separation and divorce. You worried about what was going to happen to you. You feared being left alone and abandoned. What were your feelings and thoughts? Did you feel responsible for your parents' divorce? What did you internalize about yourself? What did you say to yourself about the divorce? How did the divorce make you feel? Did you see yourself in a different way? Did you think that if you behaved better your parents would not have gotten a divorce? Did you attempt to fix whatever was happening between your parents?

These are just a few questions that a child and/or adult may have created about a divorce. Do you see how easily it is to internalize what happens to us on the outside and dance with it on in the inside? Events, our stories and beliefs about them live inside us. Our beliefs impact us physically, mentally and emotionally and the way we act. Our beliefs can also affect the way we see ourselves, and the world.

Does Your Story Define You?

People may believe that a story is just a story and it really does not mean anything. Some may be empowered by their beliefs about their stories. So, not only do we believe our stories but we also have beliefs about them. People can get stuck in their stories and their opinions about them. Being stuck in a story is like the same music playing over and over. An individual stuck in a story may not realize that they are even stuck. They listen pay attention and respond to it. It becomes so automatic like a bad habit or the "old shoe syndrome". When certain situations happen to people, their mind replays their stories over and over again. When we believe our story, we make it real. Remember, there is nothing wrong or right about stories. Powerful beliefs create our reality. When people get stuck in believing their story, it prevents them from living their potential.

Beliefs are integrated into our filters, boundaries, perceptions, and how we see ourselves and our life. As mentioned earlier, the world of perception belongs to the perceiver. Our world is infected with our past, family history, values, culture, and beliefs. These aspects in our lives influence the ways we view and interpret our world.

Every person is distinctively unique in exceptional ways, and no one perceives the world in exactly the same as we do! The problem is not that we have, create, or tell our stories, the concern is that we believe our stories and make them real. Believing our stories can block us from the real truth. Releasing our blocks is distinguishing the truth between our beliefs and the actual event.

Reframing our thoughts, feelings, and beliefs about past events can move them forward into something positive and meaningful. We can learn from the event and move past it. When people talk their stories, journal their stories or work through their stories, they open themselves to release and move past them. Unraveling stories can impact the disentanglement regarding our self-esteem and self-value. We begin to separate the happenings in our lives from the story we created about it. "Yes, it is all true. Yes, the happening. The divorce happened."

Everything in life has a price, and so does giving up our stories. There is a cost for everything. We get one thing and give up something else. For example, we may want to be in a relationship or marriage, but in order to be in a committed partnership, we have to relinquish some of our freedom. We must compromise to be in an intimate and healthy relationship.

When Does Transformation Happen?

As awareness, we have the ability to know what is real and not real. Transformation occurs when we step out of our story. We no longer need to identify with it. We become something new. Like the moon flower, it closes every night and opens a new the next day. This flower transforms itself every day. As the caterpillar begins its transformation, it starts to eat everything in sight. The caterpillar outgrows its skin many times until it is too full to even move. As it attaches itself upside-down to a branch, it forms a chrysalis. This delicate sheath limits its freedom and protects it during the duration of the metamorphosis. Inside the cocoon, there is a gooey blob. Within this ooze, new cells appear and begin to form, as if from thin air, called imaginal cells. The imaginal cells collectively become conscious that they are creating an entirely new organism and set in motion different roles, as the butterfly begins to take form. The chrysalis becomes transparent as the butterfly matures. The butterfly emerges upside-down and embraces its empty shell with such veneration as if to say thank you to where it came from.

As we grow, evolve, and change with our stories, our world changes. We transform and become new within each shift, just like the caterpillar turns into the butterfly. Transformation impacts thoughts and feelings and may change how you think and feel. When you look at a situation differently, everything becomes new. A renewal happens the moment we become aware and realize that we are not our stories. As awareness, we have the ability to know what is real and not real. We are not the stories that we made-up. We are not anything less because of the stories and the events in our lives. There is nothing wrong with having, telling, or sharing a life story. As soon as we realize the truth, we begin to unravel and separate ourselves from it. We begin to see ourselves in a new and different way. We get to unravel beliefs that may or may not be true. Knowing and clarity gives us the truth to heal.

Can You Shift the Way You Look at Your Story?

Yes, you can separate the actual events from your story and the beliefs you have about it. You can look at this process as an opening for transformation and a window in your house of story. Imagine a window that leads to a door of opportunity, growth, and change. You can let yourself see the life event and situation in a new way. When you do, you will begin to see your story differently. Seeing your story in a new way creates an opening for you to be new, to shift and to change. In this change, you will get out of your own way as you move into what is next.

Creativity

Creativity can transform painful reactions to situations and help us to heal from traumatic life experiences. Creativity gives us a renewed strength and offers a distinctive way to give voice to difficult thoughts and feelings.

Through my own creative processes—especially with dance—I have healed old wounds with a catharsis of the heart. Dance has empowered my expression throughout my life through difficulty, challenges, transitions, grief, sadness, joy, happiness, and celebration. I have moved and expressed myself in ways that satisfied and transformed me. As creative beings, we are naturally creative unless we block or stop it in some way. Creativity is a unique experience that can expand our consciousness and human potential.

Why dance?

Research emphasizes the importance of including the body in treatment for any type of trauma. Traumatic events can trigger fear and threaten our sense of safety and well-being. Life events are stored in our body memory and the sensations can become stuck. According to dance/movement therapist Claire Moore, "the sensations and actions that have become stuck in and after a traumatic event need to be integrated in the treatment process so that the person can regain a sense of familiarity and efficacy in the body." Studies have shown that dance in particular can decrease anxiety and boost mood more than other physical outlets.

Writing and Dance Reflection

What was an impacting life event? Did this event change how I see myself?

_____

_____

What story did I create from the event?

_____

_____

What did I make it mean?

_____

_____

How can I release the story?

_____

_____

How will I change when I release my story?

_____

_____

Draw a picture of your story. Be creative There are no rules in expressive dance or art!

Write about your drawing.

_____

_____

Take a good look at your drawing. What do you see?

_____

_____

How is your drawing different from your story? How is it the same?

_____

_____

Do you see anything new? How do you see yourself? If so, please explain.

_____

_____

Draw your house of story with windows and doors.

Can you look out the window? What do you see?

_____

_____

Can you open the door in your house of story?

_____

_____

What happens when you open the door?

_____

_____

What happens when you step outside the door of your house of story?

_____

_____

So you feel uncomfortable, undressed, and naked. In what ways do you feel vulnerable?

_____

_____

What do you see next for yourself? What new possibilities are you going to create?

_____

_____

Look and rewrite your story to enhance your self-esteem, value, confidence, and self-worth.

_____

_____

Dance Reflection

Dance your drawing and your story.

_____

_____

_____

_____

What message does your body and movements tell you about your story? What memories, events, issues are getting triggered from your dance and body movements?

_____

_____

12

Have a Story or Be the Real You

Letting go of stories can set you free!

This final chapter invites you to be what you truly are, a beautiful being. Would you rather have a story or be the real you?

Catharsis to Creation

Catharsis is defined as "the purging and release of relieving emotions and tensions through art, tragedy or music" (*Dictionary.com*). In the field of psychiatry, it means "encouraging and permitting and discharging pent up emotions resulting in the alleviation of symptoms or the permanent release of the condition," such as feelings, thoughts, and actions.

Catharsis is healing when we share our story with others who listen. Through communication, we reveal deep intimate parts of ourselves. We open our hearts to know what is true. We are learning to be responsible for our healing and growth.

Creative expression is a way to relieve tension, emotions, experiences, through visual arts, music, dance, singing, and all creations and crafts. Art gives us the freedom to release deep emotions and anxiety.

An art therapist told me, "Art never tells you what you already know." There is always something new that emerges from participating in artistic expression. Finger painting is a kinesthetic experience with a touch of the paints. Drawing and writing with your nondominant hand, and putting paint on one side of a paper, folding it, and then looking at it inspires creativity and gives form to what we don't know. Let art speak to you. What is your art reflecting about you? And, dance with abandon like no one is watching! You can flow with creativity and be inspired to make art, as you dance on a new journey! All you have to do is let it happen and get out of your own way!

Communication: Sharing and Conversation

Most people love talking and sharing their stories. I once asked someone, "How do I start up a conversation with someone at a networking event?" The answer was to ask the person a question about themselves. And so I did, and the conversation began! When you are ready to share your story with someone, you will know it. You will also know who, what, where, and when to communicate and tell your story. We know what to say and to whom. Listening to the still quiet voice in our hearts is our guide. This quiet, subtle voice deep within us knows. But it is not our loud ego voice that speaks first. Being at rest and calm in your heart will help you to find it and let it speak to you.

My transformation happened listening to the quiet, inner voice from within and letting it guide me. As I mentioned earlier, I let go of my life and my story as I knew it and opened my heart up to the unknown. The surface level of existence and the familiarity of my life changed, and the future was unknown. I followed and listened to the quiet voice within and let it guide me into what was next. Whether, I liked or did not like what my knowing was guiding and telling me, I followed it. I paid the price and did it anyway.

Attachments

Dictionary.org defines *attachment* as "the tendency of human infants and animals to become emotionally close to certain individuals and to be calm and soothed while in their presence." Human infants develop strong emotional bonds with a caregiver, particularly a parent, and attachment to their caregivers is a step toward establishing a feeling of security in the world." An emotional bond is formed between human infants and their caregivers, who provide comfort and security to the infant. As adults, we develop attachments based upon our earliest childhood emotional bonds. These attachments can be the emotional and supportive relationships with those that we love. Humans have a natural tendency toward attaching and bonding with someone or something. We also become attached to our stories without even realizing it. Stories nurture us in some way, whether they are joyful or painful, they comfort us. This is one of the reasons our stories are difficult to release. The attachments we have to them can make it challenging to live our lives without them. We feel naked without having them to tell, share, make excuses, and avoid responsibility.

Heartaches

Know that pain is part of the growing process. Pain is like a can opener that digs down into the deepest parts of who we are. Know that there will be pain in letting go of your attachments. Know that pain is okay and that you are okay in letting go of your story. Know that pain does not hurt you, it just doesn't feel very good. Know that everything is there to help you evolve. Pain can be present when we release and let go of attachments to thoughts, feelings, emotions, people, relationships, places, material possessions, and stories. Our attachments are our comforts, and when we let them go, we feel uncomfortable. It is like being a child and not wanting to let go of your bottle, a toy, or your blanket. Releasing what we are used to and letting it go can hurt. Know that it is only pain and you can be okay with it. What story are you attached to?

List any other attachments you may have in your life, such as people, places, and things.

What story is comforting to you? When you are honest, which story do you need to release for your well-being? Some stories are more difficult to release than others. And, you know which ones you have to release. How can you make letting go of this story easy? Listen to the quiet voice within for the answer.

My personal story of letting go of the life I knew was difficult and painful. I realized how attached I was to my personal possessions, such as my house, dog, car, the antique furniture, and things, people in my life, and my job. I experienced the pain of being attached to many things. In order to move to Maui, I knew had to give up my possessions, because I could not afford to take them across the ocean. I cried a lot and grieved the loss of my things!

In the catharsis of your story, you choose and are willing to let go. Your will, habits, preferences, beliefs, and patterns can take you down the road of having and keeping your story, or you can choose to let go.

Sharing a secret story can be cathartic and healing. In telling your story, healing can happen from releasing pent-up emotions and old wounds. When you open your heart and speak your story to someone willing to listen, you invite the possibility of a new way of seeing the event. Do you want to have a story or be the real you? Letting go of your story is to choose to step into the unknown!

Know the Difference between Being and Having

We live in the world of *having*. This world is filled with the consumption of materials and getting and buying things. What is in it for me? Why should I do this? What will I get from it? One of the greatest distractions in the world, is fulfilling our wants and needs. The truth is as consumers, there will always be more to get and have. It is like an unfulfilled prophecy. We are beings, not the haves or have nots (like the television show). As human beings we can choose to be free and be, or we can keep holding on to *having* our story. You get to choose.

How can we move from having, wanting and getting to being in the moment? Be still in the quietness of your heart. Relax your body. Know that there is nothing to get or do. Beingness is not a doing. Be open and soft in your heart. When we are quiet, as stillness, we can listen. Nature is a great teacher. Nature knows who we are, and speaks to us when we listen. Enjoy being with nature. You may be inspired to hug a tree. Enjoy being in the moment.

The world sends a different message of how to be. The message is that you are a human doing instead of a human being. The world tells us to *do* instead of to *be*. Moving from "doing" to "being" can be a challenging and difficult step. It is different way of being in the world.

Every day, you are responsible for doing your daily work, chores, tasks, responsibilities, obligations, and the list goes on and on. Rewriting your story does not imply that you are giving up in doing all your responsibilities in life. You are learning to be new in your life. Learning to be in the moment can take practice. This may take time if you are used to running and doing things on a daily basis. You are changing your way of being. Pay close attention to the simple baby steps you are taking to relax and be.

You are being in the moment. You are not taking life for granted or expecting anything, you are being aware of what is happening right now. Relax your body and be quiet and still. With practice, you can learn to not need anything, get anything, go anywhere, or have anything. You can experience your *beingness* right now. Knowing that you can do it will motivate you to practice. Take time every day to learn how to be. Let your inner knowing guide you. One day you may want to sit by a river or on top of a mountain or smell a flower. Or, you may discover some new insights about yourself in learning how to be. Take a moment to be quiet and still every day.

Dancing is my passion. I love being in my body and moving. When I hear music, my body starts to move! History tells us that the earliest identity of human beings was dance. When one tribal member would met another, they would ask" What do you dance?" Is dancing in our human DNA? I think so. One of the first things an infant does is move to the sound of music. A baby naturally dances and moves to music. I enjoy dancing with my inner flow as I harmonize to my own rhythm. I can be upset having a bad day, or not feeling well, and I will always have more energy, gain clarity, and feel better after dancing!

Recent research has discovered more health benefits of dance in addition to stress reduction and increased serotonin level, with its sense of well-being. Scientific evidence has proven that frequent dancing makes you smarter. Dance also increases cognitive acuity at all ages!

Now I know there is a scientific reason I experience a feeling of well-being and mental clarity after dancing. I enjoy creative expression and engage in activities such as writing, painting, cooking, gardening, collages, decorating and entrepreneurship.

Authenticity

Being authentic means being genuine and true. The more you release your stories, the more real you will become. You will be free because you don't have to pretend anymore! There is more space for the real you and less stories to clutter your awareness and seeing.

My personal experiences took me on a journey to realize that what was happening to me was helping me to become more authentic. Then, I became open to the process of growing and evolving. Even though it was excruciatingly painful at times I began to enjoy the process. Let honesty guide you in knowing and seeing. This may be a painful process, but it is worth it! The pain of releasing the past propelled me forward as I let go of my stories. My parent story hindered me from being true to myself for most of my life. I lived my victim story instead of choosing powerfully to release it. Now, I feel a sense of freedom and well-being knowing that my parents made their choices and I did too. I choose to live my life to the fullest as a "more seasoned" human being.

How can you be more authentic and true to yourself? What story do you need to review and/or rewrite? When will you commit release this story, accept the event/situation circumstance as is, learning from it, and moving forward?

I let go of this story_____

I accept_____

I know_____as a result of this experience

I commit to _____and free myself to move forward.

I am authentic because _____

Creative Expression

Creativity is a wonderful journey for self-expression, catharsis, and the realization of the unknown. There is a spark of creativity in everyone. The creative process triggers the past and experiences stored deep in the subconscious. This occurs when we step aside, let it happen and flow with creativity. Art stimulates the brain and the imagination. Art can make you more observant and see new things as well as help you to problem-solve. Creativity can also reduce stress, enhance self-esteem, and improve cognitive functioning. Art tells the truth, and art reveals something new. Doing art to help recreate your story can be fun and enjoyable. Express yourself through creativity and the arts. Being creative can help you move through your story with an artistic flare.

Pay attention when you are doing your art, whether it is painting, sculpting, making collages, photography, and drawing. Remember to focus on being creative and the satisfaction of making art, not the product and end result. Throughout the process, you may experience a variety of thoughts and feelings. These may include happiness, sadness, depression, fears, anxiety, a sense of hopefulness, your failures and triumphs, and personal issues.

Artistic Discovery

Look for images in your artwork. What do you see? Art can be like dreams communicating from your unconscious. In teaching a visual arts class, I had students doing scribbling and then had them looking for their portrait in the scribble. In an abstract piece, one student found his father, who had passed away, and he had been grieving the loss. Creative expression invites you down an unfamiliar path. You never know what you may find in the creative process. Nurture yourself through creative expression.

Dance and move in the freedom of being you!

Creative Imagination

Creative exploration can be a great tool to explore your inner story. Imagine what you would be like without your story. What would your life look like? How would you be and act? Draw or write it out. Set your imagination free to roam and discover new insights about you and your life.

Journaling

You can release emotions, feelings, thoughts, dramas, shame, guilt, and fear by writing in a journal every day. It is amazing what pen and paper can do for your health! You can be inspired with new and fresh ideas. There are many health benefits associated with writing every day. Journaling can strengthen your immune system, and writing about stressful events can help you to come to terms with them. It also helps reduce the impact of these stressors on you physical, emotional, and mental health and well-being. Scientific evidence supports that journaling accesses your left brain, which is analytical and rational. While your left brain is free to create, intuit, and feel. Writing removes mental blocks and allows you to use all of your brainpower to better understand yourself, others, and the world around you. Journaling can clarify thoughts and feelings, reduce stress, help you to learn more about yourself, find solutions to problems, and resolve issues with others.

The Artist's Way, a book by Julia Cameron, recommends writing morning pages every day. The *Artist's Way* is a powerful and inspiring work of art that takes readers on an amazing twelve-week journey to discover the link between their spiritual and creative selves. The two pivotal tools in creative discovery and recovery are the morning pages and the artist date. Connecting with our inner creativity can be beneficial in rewriting your story. You can write about your story in your morning pages and be creative with it. The morning pages are written daily for the weeks of the course. The morning pages are three handwritten pages written in longhand in a stream-of-consciousness style. You may begin writing down that you have nothing to write. Challenge yourself to see what comes up in your writing. Give your hand the freedom to stream in being conscious of your writing. Remember there is no right or wrong way to do your morning pages! Nothing is too petty, unreasonable, too silly, stupid, or weird! Julia Cameron emphasizes the importance of writing in longhand. Writing in longhand slows us down and enables us to connect to our emotions and intuitions. We can act in holistic ways that reflect the integrated whole aspects of yourself. We live in an instant world, but fast is not always better. Writing by hand is like driving slowly down a street and seeing all of our surroundings. We become aware of our thoughts, feelings, and physical sensations when writing.

When I do my journal pages, I never know what I am going to write. I just let my hand and pen flow. I let my writing tell me what I need to know, instead of the other way around. You put your questions on the top of the page and let your writing tell you the answer too! Whichever way works for you is perfect. The most important rule is that there are no rules!

In focusing on the process not the product, the end result, your focal point changes. You can relax without worrying how your piece, project, or writing is going to look or turn out. Put your inner critic away and engage in the creative process. Enjoy seeing what develops and is being communicated to you. Let yourself see the truth about the piece of art. Embrace the message in the artistic expression and learn from what the art is telling you. Art always tell you something new. Listening your inner knowing can guide and assist you through the creative process. Painting, sculpting, drawing, and photography are relaxing and rewarding hobbies that help to rewrite a story, reduce stress, and enhance well-being.

Dancing with Your Story from Victim to Victory

As human beings, it is our nature to create stories and become good storytellers. Everyone has a story, and everyone tells it well. We have stories about ourselves, our family, friends, business, career, workplace, relationships, and much more. If your situation happened to someone else, would they see or interpret it the same way that you do? Would you embrace the story with acceptance and without judgment?

The tendency for human beings to be egocentric can give us an edge in the way we see our world. We have the natural inclination to see others differently, which includes our stories. For example, in seeing our stories subjectively, we may consider ourselves to be the victims of our stories or blame others. If the same situation happened to someone else, would we blame them for it? When life happens, we see it through our own eyes in our own way. It is so automatic that we may not even be aware that we are doing it.

The framework of a life event as a story is powerful, because once we realize we created a story, we can change it! Dance in the realization that a life event has become a story. And, know that we have the power to recreate it and let it go. It is an opportunity for personal development and growth. When we step out of our story, it means stepping into something new. Stepping out of our story can be a life-changing occurrence or very subtle. The shift can affect the way we see ourselves, our life, and others, whether it feels big or small. Changing our stories and letting them go can be a life-altering event. Life happens in a variety of ways, and the way we react and respond to life is also diverse and unique. Someone else's experience may or may not be the same as our response.

Dancing in a new story and moving forward into the unknown can be easy or difficult. You get to choose. Know that it is okay, either way. We can have growing pains forward or be open and enjoy the the journey. The way we perceive our story is the way we perceive changing it or letting it go. It can be challenging, and it can also trigger emotions such as fear, discomfort, and an unwillingness to change. The walls of resistance may also arise when we begin to change in a new and better way. We can fight, and be in conflict with ourselves. Or we can choose to move with grace and ease.

Remember, the problem is not our stories, it is our beliefs about them. What we believe to be true becomes our reality. Sometimes we would rather stick to our story and stay stuck in it than change and move into the new. We prefer to do the same things the same way. The unfamiliar can be scary, and it frightens us into keeping our old ways and stepping back into our story!

Are You Playing the Blame-and-Shame Game?

The blame-and-shame game involves us pointing the finger at others and blaming and shaming them for our stories. When we place blame on others, we are not taking full responsibility for our own thoughts, feelings, and actions. When we place shame on others, we dishonor them. And, in the process, we dishonor ourselves. We are making them wrong. When we place blame or shame on another regarding our stories, we are not being responsible. We are not victims of our stories. Instead of blaming, we can ask ourselves: What did that other person give to us? And how are we a better human being because of this relationship? We are responsible human beings in our lives.

Avoid playing the blame-and-shame game with yourself also. You are an adult taking responsibility of your actions toward moving forward with your life. Know that we are all a piece of artwork in progress. Always be loving, gentle, kind, and patient with yourself. Love yourself for reviewing and reliving your story and the life event. Avoid blaming and shaming or dishonoring yourself with unkind words or self-abuse. Love yourself!

Shame is the feeling that there is something wrong with us. We may point the finger and blame others when we do not want to take responsibility for ourselves and our life. We may feel there is something wrong with us instead of thinking that we may have made a mistake. Be okay with yourself exactly the way you are. Self-love is also important for our health and well-being. Loving all the aspects of ourselves means accepting things what we like and do not like about ourselves in a caring, nurturing, and gentle kind of way. We know that we must love ourselves first before we can really love someone else. Describe the ways in which you can accept yourself exactly the way you are. How can you nurture and love yourself? Our stories did not create us, we created our stories.

As human storytellers, we make stories so naturally, not even realizing that we are creating them. Can you see how easy it is to internalize what happens to us on the outside and take it on in the inside? We can easily make the events in our lives live inside of us. Not only do the events live inside us, but the thoughts and feelings too. They become the foundation for our beliefs. We believe the way we think and feel about ourselves. Internalizing our story impacts and affects our self-esteem and self-worth.

* * * * *

Within our life story is the framework for our beliefs about us. Think back to your earliest memories as a child. What do you remember? What do you remember saying to yourself? What did you make the event mean to you? Can you describe the ways you internalized this event? How did you make it a part of you?

In telling, sharing, and rewriting our stories, we relive them. Stories that are based upon our life events are painful and cause suffering. But the truth is, rewriting our story is an opportunity to let ourselves heal from our life event. In order to rewrite our story, we have to let ourselves see the life event in a different way. We reframe it in a new and different way. If we have blamed someone else for our painful experiences from a past relationship, and we let ourselves see the truth that we were also responsible for the break up or divorce, then we can heal the past and have a fresh start with ourselves and our lives. We learn to take full responsibility and ownership for ourselves and our lives.

Many painful childhood circumstances were not in our control. As adults, we realize that we can protect and heal ourselves. I have learned to relate to my abandonment issues as an adult in a new and healthier way. But know that we are not victims, even though we may have been victimized in life situations, conditions, and events. Remember, be okay that the event happened. We can be okay that the abuse or event happened even though we know that the individual's actions were not okay.

When we open ourselves to knowing this truth, healing happens. When we clean and clear out the old cobwebs of pain, judgment, fear, and experiences and let in the new ideas and experiences, we heal.

We all have been witness to unbelievable stories of survival after years of horrible experiences. Know that you too are a survivor and can move past your story. If you are open and willing to take the journey into unknown, face your fears with courage, and rewrite your story, then you can transform yourself and your life in the process. There is nothing wrong with having, a life story, but it is better to be the real you!

- *Life Event Perceptions*
  What are your perceptions about the life event?
  Describe the ways you perceive the event through your senses, feelings, emotions, and observations.
  How are your perceptions of the event keeping you from being the real you?

- *Beliefs*
  What do you believe to be true about the event based on your perceptions?
  What are your beliefs?
  What beliefs are you willing to change about the event?
  How are your beliefs keeping you stuck in your story?

- *Meaning*
  What does what happened or the event mean to you?
  What do you want to make it mean?
  Whatever happened is real, what you make it mean is not. For example, you experience something unpleasant at work. Your boss offers you corrective criticism on your job performance. You make it mean you are not good at your job or you do not like your job any longer. Neither of these is true. You put the meaning on the event that occurred

at the workplace. The fact and the truth of the matter are simple. Your boss offered you constructive criticism.

- *Change*

   What changes can you make about the meaning you gave about your story?

   How can you take full responsibility for the life event? Change happens by taking full responsibility for ourselves ourselves and our lives. Taking full responsibility for this example could be to accept the criticism as a way of becoming better and improving at the workplace. Be grateful and open to your boss's criticism about your work performance. By improving and listening and making the necessary changes, you may earn a raise. What changes do you need to make to be free of your story and be the real you?

Writing and Dance Reflection

What is the main story you have been working on throughout this book?

_____

_____

What story is keeping you from being the real you? How can you rewrite and release your story?

_____

_____

Describe three ways that letting go of your story/stories will give you the freedom to choose powerfully.

_____

_____

_____

What will your transformation look like when release your story?

_____

_____

What did you learn about yourself from the release of your stories?

_____

_____

Describe how you will love and accept yourself exactly the way you are.

_____

_____

Imagine transforming out of your cocoon into a beautiful butterfly. What color are your wings? Describe how it feels to fly and flitter and enjoy the nectar of flowers and be free.

_____

_____

Dance Reflection

Let your body relax and freely move to your favorite music. Dance and imagine coming out of a cocoon. Being free. Move in the ways a butterfly moves and dances in the air. Fly and flutter your wings. Enjoy the freedom and nectar of the flowers all around you!

Write about your transformational dance and movement experiences.

_____

_____

_____

_____

The Butterfly Effect

You are like a butterfly that is ready to fly out of the cocoon and dance for the first time. Be like a butterfly with the freedom to fly. Let the metamorphosis of change and growth set you free to be new. Accept and release the stories in your life that no longer serve you. Know that you are a being on a journey of change and evolution. All that you were before no longer serves you. Be grateful and appreciate all of your experiences, be it joyous or painful. Dance and celebrate your gifts. Transform into the beautiful being that you are. Enjoy the dance as you evolve and become the most beautiful butterfly ever!!

About the Author

"The greatest gift that I know is to follow what I know with courage confidence and trust." Following one's passion means being fearless and having faith and creative intelligence—an awesome combination for living life to the fullest! Passion comes from a zest and vigor for loving oneself and a willingness to pay the price.

Arielle's passions include dance, psychology, philosophy, writing, and the creative arts. She dances through life as an international and inspirational author, dancer, choreographer, teacher, painter, and facilitator who inspires her audience.

Arielle has a masters of arts degree in counselor education and in educational leadership. As faculty member and lead faculty area chairperson for the college of humanities, history, and the arts at the University of Phoenix, she has inspired students with her profound knowledge of Humanities, Art, Psychology and Philosophy. She has studied philosophy at the College of Integrated Philosophy with John DeRuiter for eighteen years.

She is a published author of several books and *Tampa Bay Wellness and Transformation* magazine articles. In 2014, she published her fourth book, an instructor's manual for *Barlow Abnormal Psychology* (Fourth edition). In 2013, she cowrote *Psychology: A Journey* (Third edition), a study guide published by Nelson Education.

Arielle has been a featured guest on radio and television shows, in newspapers, and other media across the United States and Canada. She offers dance classes, dancing from the inside out workshops, creative expression seminars, for children and adults.

www.dancingfromtheinsideout.com

Made in the USA
Columbia, SC
25 September 2017